PROPHETS OF JOY

D0596719

Prophets of Joy

A SPIRITUALITY FOR THE BAPTIZED

"Listen anyone who has ears to hear" (LUKE 14:35)

Jean Miller
Daughter of Charity

Sheed & Ward
London

Nihil obstat Anton Cowan, Censor
Imprimatur †John Crowley, V.G., Bishop in Central London,
  Westminster, 5 May 1989

ISBN 0 7220 6970 7

First published in 1989 by Sheed & Ward Ltd
2 Creechurch Lane, London EC3A 5AQ
Filmset by Waveney Typesetters, Norwich
Printed and bound in Great Britain
by BPCC Wheatons Ltd, Exeter

Book production by Bill Ireson

NA-3198

Contents

1. So What? 1

Part I: *God's Plan* 5

2. Worlds within Worlds 6
3. Wider Horizons 10
4. Fireworks 13
5. The Time Machine 18
6. Christkind 23
7. Fill my House unto the Fullest 27

Part II: *God's Word on Earth* 31

8. Paving the Way 32
9. Pathfinding 37
10. Bridges 42
11. Out of the Mist 49
12. Spirit-filled 54
13. One more Station 60

Part III: *God's Adopted Children* 67

14. Echoes 68
15. Smog 72
16. A Drop of Water 76
17. Christopher 83
18. Hand-in-Hand 88

CONTENTS

19.	Off-centre	93
20.	Soap and Water	97
21.	A Crumb of Bread	101
22.	Conkers	107
23.	Profit and Loss	112
24.	Aunt Sally	116
25.	Into the Depths	120
26.	Fall-out	124
27.	Just Waiting	129

List of Illustrations

Page

As Creation took shape, and stars, planets and star-dust of all   14
kinds fell into the places God had assigned for them, the Spirit
of God hovered over the handiwork of the Word uttered by the
Godhead, and our world came into being. This world of men
and women that "God so loved that he would give his only Son
that all might have eternal life"

What is creation? A Word of God uttered into the immensity of   24
nothingness. And God, the God of love, God who *is* Love, so
loved this Word spoken from all eternity, that into this created
world "God sent his only Son" and the Word became man, the
man Jesus. Jesus is in the world and "his fullness fills the whole
creation" as he draws all humankind unto himself so that all may
have eternal life

No one can draw a picture of Spirit, no one can draw God. We   43
can merely use symbols that speak to us of God. God is
everywhere in heaven and on earth. There is no distance for
God. The lightning that flashes across the heavens or rips the sky
apart is but a feeble image of the Word of God who, at a
moment in time, "leapt into the heart" of creation, into "that
doomed land" so needing a Saviour for having turned away from
the Word of its Creator. "God so loved the world that he gave
his only Son so that everyone who believes in him may not be
lost but may have eternal life" (John 3:16)

Plunged into the waters of Baptism humankind is united to the   77
death of Christ, and then, sharing his Resurrection, is raised to a
higher life and is taken into the life of the Trinity as adopted sons
and daughters. The eternal light of God, symbolized by the sun,
shines upon the newly baptized. This was made possible by the
death of the Son upon a tree. And, once more, the Spirit of Love

is there, hovering over our divine adoption for "God so loved the world" that the Son died upon the tree so that the light of God might shine upon us eternally

Men and women inhabit this world, the work of the Creator.   102
They till the soil and harness the forces of nature so that by the labour of all things created they may have food to sustain their God-given life. But the true life that God gives is greater than just their human life, needing bread. The higher, divine life, which is theirs as adopted daughters and sons of God, also requires nourishment, the Bread of Life. This Bread is the Body and Blood of Christ, that Jesus Christ the only Son of God who was sent into this world so that we might have eternal life. So God willed, for God so loved the world

This book is dedicated to
Sister Louisa Mary Bankes, S.N.D
with gratitude and love

Biblical quotations are from the *Jerusalem Bible* unless otherwise indicated, and are used with permission of the publishers, Darton, Longman & Todd Ltd.

Royalties earned from the sale of this book are being donated by the author to help the work of the Sisters of Charity in Lebanon.

Introduction

Many years ago I trained as a teacher in Mount Pleasant College, Liverpool. Our RE lecturer was Sister Louisa Mary Bankes. One day she set us an essay the subject of which was: "Comment upon, 'In me Christ lives, prays and suffers'". I set about the task and, to the best of my ability, filled as many pages as I thought necessary, and handed in my work.

A few days later Sister Louisa Mary called me. I forget the words she used but the message was clear: "You've missed the whole point. You just haven't a clue." She then gave me a beautiful explanation. Again I have forgotten her words but their meaning I never forgot. It was a breakthrough to realms I had never dreamed of. From then on I searched, I read, I reflected and I meditated the mystery that Sister Louisa Mary had unfolded to me.

In many ways *Prophets of Joy* is a rewrite of that essay of long ago.

CHAPTER ONE

So What?

"How awful!" I said as I stood in front of a large painting in a church some years ago. The artist had intended to represent the coronation of the Blessed Virgin. God the Father stood woodenly at one side. He had long white hair and substantial beard and was dressed in a white soutane, like some old-time missionary. The Son was rather like the usual pictures of the Sacred Heart, and the Holy Spirit fluttered above, the classical dove. On a very straight chair sat Mary, stiff and solemn. Her Son was holding a massive crown above her head. Nothing could have been less convincing nor less appealing. "How awful!" I repeated sadly.

The awful thing about it was that all of this symbolized the rigid, formal, impersonal, institutional concept of religion that has been all too prevalent. Perhaps this explains why so many people have fallen away from the Church, and why so many young people will have none of it.

I will have none of that kind of religion either. I am not a theologian but a plain Christian who, rejecting all that smug narrowness, have been thinking through my faith to see what I do believe, and believe in strongly. There is no point in being a "Faint half-believer of a casual creed" (Matthew Arnold). And, having checked to make sure that I wasn't just inventing a creed of my own, I thought that perhaps sharing all this with you might help you to think through your faith a little more clearly too.

To me faith is not a question of classified articles for belief and laws to be obeyed – they are there, yes, but that is the wrong end to start from. To me religion is a glorious and loving relationship with God. A relationship that God took the initiative in wanting, and planned from all eternity. "We are to love then, because he loved us first" (1 John 4:19).

That means that there never was a moment when God didn't think of me and want me, desire me, I might even say, for God is Love. Love is the motive behind all the divine plans, the element in which they thrive and the end which is their fulfilment. It is because of this that, although I might sometimes seem to enjoy myself or even have a whale of a time, if it is outside of God, my pleasure is only short-lived and is not deep-seated happiness. Basically I am not happy, and never will be, without God, outside of God. "Thou hast made us for thyself, Oh Lord, and our hearts will never rest until they rest in thee" (St Augustine).

I said that God planned this relationship, so what I am examining is what this plan was, how God brought it about, and is still bringing it about, and where you and I come into the picture. It seems to make sense that if it is God's plan it will only work if we accept it on God's terms.

That God is Love is marvellous, and the Bible, both Old and New Testaments, expound upon that and tell us a lot more about God and the divine purpose in creating anything at all. All this is very exciting, especially as everything points to a splendid destiny being intended for us. And the way is shown how we can attain it. We learn who we are and what we are to become.

Life on earth is often complicated, problematic and puzzling. It doesn't always look as if God were particularly interested in us. Some people think that God's day is over and that we can get along very well without anything as childish as belief in God. They think that they are in charge of this earth and that they don't need, or want, any so-called divine interference. "Sin" is an old-fashioned word, and suffering a curse. Life is a dream, if not a nightmare considering all the evil we see around us, and there is only a Big Black Hole at the end. That can't be the answer! It would be too big a waste, and waste, as we all know, is very difficult to dispose of. I find that trying to dispose of God presents a very much greater problem! So what?

Well, this book will look at all that and will be concerned with both the beginning and the end of all creation and everything that happens in between. The key figure that stands out, dwarfing all else, is the person of Jesus Christ, the Word of God made man, and what he means to you and me. All this is the subject of my tale.

As this story is not a recital of lists of definitions or a code of legislation, but the tale of a wonderful relationship, it can't be slotted into neat files or recorded on alphabetical index cards. Relationships are living and free, and involve situations of all kinds, but there is a thread, a golden thread which runs through this tale. It is the tale of a God of immense love, who created a marvellous universe, out of love, and for that love. A love that has a name, the "Word of God", a love who is the centre of all creation and into whom all creation is ultimately drawn, drawn into unending life, the glorious love-life of Godself. Believe me, it is a very thrilling, rich, warm and beautiful story that I have to tell, every page pointing prophetically to the immense joy God has in store for us.

Part I: *God's Plan*

"He has let us know the mystery of his purpose, the hidden plan he made so kindly in Christ from the beginning" (Ephesians 1:9).

God spoke and the Eternal Word of God brought into being the many great marvels of creation that we see about us. This was not accidental or capricious but according to a plan.

"The Word that goes forth from my mouth does not return to me empty, without carrying out my will and succeeding in what it was sent to do" (Isaiah 55:11).

The High point of Creation was Jesus, the Word of God made man. Jesus was to carry out the will God had in creating, in sending forth "the Word from my mouth", and he would return to God bearing as trophies of his victories "whole hordes for his tribute" (Isaiah 53:12) which he will have "drawn unto himself" (cf. John 12:32).

But would people know this? Or would they shut themselves up in small mundane concerns and fail to recognize their great Creator in the world around them, in each other and in the Christ-Church that the Son of God established upon earth?

Part I of this book is designed to help people make the discovery of the Creator and of Christ.

CHAPTER TWO

Worlds within Worlds

I went on holiday one year with a group of children to Holy Island, off the coast of Northumbria. At high tide it really is an island but at low tide it is connected to the mainland by a causeway. We spent most of the day on the beach, picnic meals and all.

One particular day the tide was out exposing slushy wet sand, stretches of rough, flat rocks and masses of sea-weed. Flocks of sea-birds were circling around looking for food in the shallow water and wet sand, and three children were crouching, spellbound at the edge of a tiny pool in the hollow of some rocks.

It was a very, very tiny pool but it was a little world of wonders. The bottom was carpeted with pale yellow sand. Seaweed of different shades of green decorated the sides. A little starfish lay on the bed of sand among lovely little shells of various shapes and sizes. Some of the shells were inhabited and moved as the minute living beings inside them walked around their domain. A few baby crabs scuttled about and some shrimp-like little creatures swam in and out between the multicoloured stones and pebbles that furnished the pond. On the surrounding rocks limpets stuck fast. Shut in by their own shells they would never even see God's world of wonders just at their front doors. They would stay there until some bird broke their shells with its beak or a child smashed them with a stone.

The three children just gazed. One little boy soon grew tired of gazing. There was nothing he could get from the pond – nothing to be gained. The little girl thought that "it was very pretty" but her interest soon waned too. The third child, however, a little boy, was something of a scientist, and perhaps a bit of a philosopher and theologian as well. He just couldn't look enough.

I couldn't read what was going on in that young head but, knowing the child, I imagine that in some way, perhaps very vaguely and inexplicitly, he saw God in that little pool. Far more sensitive than the other lad and more profound than the girl, he was making calculations and marvelling.

Did he notice the pitiful narrowness of the limpet's life, just stuck to the rock, shut out from all around, even the light of the sun, by its own tight fitting shell? Did he muse on the beauty of the starfish, so perfect in form, colour and detail of every kind, even the geometrical exactitude of the positioning of its five points? Maybe he noted the instinctive fear of the baby crabs hastily scuttling to the precarious safety of the underside of a stone when he gently poked at them with a piece of sea-weed. Did he reflect on the shortness of the lives of all the creatures of the pool, and how life went on there oblivious of any wider horizons, ignorant even of the life going on in the next pool, just a few feet away? Did he ponder on the meaning of it all – where it all came from, and what next? Little boy, "Greater things than this you will see" (John 1:50).

The tide was coming in, soon the pool, and the many others like it, would be covered by the sea, and the life within it would be buffeted by the waves rolling over the rocks and up the beach. Besides, it was tea-time and the three children joined their friends for a picnic on the sand dunes.

While I sat munching sandwiches my eyes roamed round the stretch of coast that surrounded us. From behind we were cut off by the dunes that sloped down to an expanse of white sand, shut in on one side by a rocky headland with sea-birds nesting on the ledges of its cliffs. On the other side irregular rocks jutted out to sea. On their extremities cormorants were spreading and flapping their wings. The tide had come in far enough to cover the pool that had filled us with such wonder, but here, in this bay, was a bigger and a better world. The pool was a mini-creation and beautiful, "very pretty" the girl had said. God had made the pool, yes, but God also made bigger things than pools. This stretch of sand and rocks, this great expanse of sea and sky, the blues and the browns, the whites and gold were God's. God's also were the flocks of birds, the seals whose heads bobbed up and down like big black dots far out at sea, the glorious sights and sounds, the warmth of sun and cool of breeze. All of this was God's creation, God's most wonderful world. Yet: "Greater things than this will you see."

When we got back to the village on the other side of the island the tourists had all left. The incoming tide had sent them hurrying back to the mainland, and now the island was totally cut off, a world of its own. This is the way the islanders like it. Their little world at peace. There is no sign of the rat-race here. Fishermen and farmers quietly go about their unhurried business, rabbits run about the dunes unmolested, the wind whistles through the long, coarse grass, and the ruins of the old priory stand out black against the evening sky.

Holy Island really is a world of its own, a peaceful, nostalgic world where gentle ghosts chant vespers in the evening breeze, and sea-birds of every feather find sanctuary. A holy world indeed, a world of God's unspoilt wilderness where everywhere can be heard "the sound of Yahweh walking in the garden at the cool of day" (Genesis 3:8).

Wild, unspoilt places like this exist in many parts of the world. Pools of loveliness that have been left behind when the tide of time went out. Idyllic spots where the human spirit can also stand still, and hear: "Come away to some lonely place all by yourselves and rest a while" (Mark 6:31). And we feel like crying out like Peter, "It is wonderful for us to be here . . . let us pitch our tents" (Matthew 17:4), for surely this is paradise.

God's plan, however, was not a static one. Eden was not the end-all. Anyway it would soon have become too boring for words. Perhaps there is a hint of that in the story of Eve picking the forbidden fruit – there would be something new, and she would, so she was told, be in a position of command. God did indeed mean humankind to control their environment: "Fill the earth and conquer it. Be masters of the fish of the sea, the birds of the heaven and all the living animals on earth" (Genesis 1:28); "Yahweh God took the man and settled him in the garden of Eden to cultivate and take care of it" (Genesis 2:15). Holy Island and other beautiful and peaceful spots are indeed part of God's world but, "Greater things than this will you see," and the co-operation of human beings is required in bringing this about.

CHAPTER THREE

Wider Horizons

Standing on the hillock overlooking the stretch of water that separated the island from the mainland it was hard to believe that anyone could ever get across dry shod, that there could be a causeway a few miles long linking the two worlds. Two entirely different worlds they certainly were. Behind me a world of rocks and sand, long grass and wild flowers, of fish, rabbits and birds, a world of sun and wind and lashing rain, a world of peace and childhood's primordial innocence. In front, across that water, were hubbub and competition, media, progress, invention and bustle. The distance between the two worlds was more than just a step forward, it symbolized for me a gigantic leap ahead; something similar to what scientists would call a "mutation" – an advance to an entirely new form of creation, for example, such as took place when first plant life, then animal life, appeared on earth, and even more so when men and women first stood erect, conscious of themselves and able to reflect. Is there a further leap up to higher things to come? I think there is. We will see.

The next day our mini-bus took us across the causeway. Hardly had we reached the mainland than our road was blocked by the gates of a level crossing. Seconds later an express roared past. Speed and noise, noise and speed hit us like a shock, only to be repeated when, a couple of hundred yards further on, we turned into a main road and we, ourselves, became part of the rushing flow of traffic heading for the bigger world of work and daily living – the adult world of men and women, today's people with their technology and complicated organization. The media world where television and telex flash the latest news of cup matches, scandals and terrorist activities, in the first, second and third worlds, into every home. A busy world, a progressive world, a heavily-weighted world, often a wicked and corrupt world, a rat-race world.

There's an uncomfortable feeling about this rat-race world, though there are those who dismiss it with an attitude of, "Well, that's life." To them it doesn't seem to matter that might is often right and the weakest go to the wall. And if any of these weakest try to hit back they are thought of, and treated, as "baddies". We can't dismiss it nor ever forget it.

However, there is another side to the world where men and women are striving for peace and justice. This world, this adult world of men and women is God's world even if not everyone knows it. Because it is God's world it is a searching world, a world of ideals and dreams. A brave struggling world of ambition, discovery, invention, vision and love. God's big, wonderful world.

Many people do not know that what they are ultimately searching for is God. Neither do they realize that in all their striving, loving, inventing and discovery they are, in reality, co-operating with the Almighty Godself in building up, and up, and up, the divine work of creation. But all too often we stop short of the final leap up to that life where God is to be found and so much of our searching, striving and toiling are in vain. So long as that is the case the rat-race world will never be transformed, as only God can bring about a transformation, but we must co-operate with God.

Some of us seek only our own personal gain or advantage. Some are impressed by surface effects but do not look any deeper. But then there are also the scientists and the theologians who delve profoundly into the mysteries of God's creation, and cannot look enough.

Not everyone is interested in the marvels the scientists and theologians tell us. Many of us are just plain short-sighted. Our worlds are as limited as the little rock pool and our vision stretches no further. Even so, we are still in God's world, because God's world is everywhere, but we are in it in much the same way as the limpet is, stuck to its rock, so we do not enjoy it to the full and the god we know – if any – is a very small god cut down to the size of our narrow world, not a god who loves us and has so much to offer us. If this is our case, no wonder if, like the little boy and girl on the beach, we soon lose interest.

A good question at this point is: "In what size world do *I* live?" Is it a rock pool or outer space? Whichever it is I can find God there but, of course, if I only live in a pool my vision of God is likely to be rather restricted and I probably won't pay much heed to such a petty deity. But the God of outer space as well as of the pool is a God to be reckoned with, a Power I can trust in, a God I can adore, a God I can love because that God loved me first. So I can either shut my eyes and block my ears and turn in upon myself and shrink and shrink and shrink, or I can open up every particle of my being and let God in.

Then I shall see God's reflection in every sun-set and dew drop, in every butterfly and bird and child, yes, in every man and woman standing upright, head erect, or bent low with suffering, deprivation, addiction or shame – awaiting transformation. God's presence suffusing the whole creation, the world and the whole majestic cosmos so that everything within the universe pulses with divine life. But still the question looms within me: "Why? Why all these marvels of creation? Why me? How did it all start? What is the purpose and where are we all going? And are there still 'greater things that we will see'?"

CHAPTER FOUR

Fireworks

Everyone loves a firework show. One after another the rockets speed into the evening sky, and with a "bang" give birth to a shower of multicoloured sparks that float a little, then fall like shooting stars before disappearing into the night.

Perhaps God likes something of that sort too. In any case scientists tell us that all these worlds within worlds that make up God's universe began with a "Big Bang", and that myriads of stars were born of that "Big Bang". Not only stars but masses of rock, gasses, nuclei or whatever, that formed planets and other heavenly bodies. I'm not a scientist, but I think they say that it may have been a piece broken off one of the molten masses, then cooled, that finally formed our Earth. Only it wasn't the Earth as we know it now. It was a kind of dead chaos which gradually evolved – over millions of years – into a recognizable structure of land and sea. Out of this sea gradually, very gradually, evolved first plants and minute creatures, then trees and beasts and birds, and finally humankind, God's master-piece. Yes, even you and me.

The only thing is, they can't tell us a great deal about what made that Big Bang, or why, or what was before. Theologians tell us that it was God who created the whole universe and all that is in it, out of nothing, by a word. The Bible says that God created the world and all it contains: "Look at the heavens and the earth and see all that is in them, and know that God has made them from nothing, and that the human race came to be in that way" (2 Maccabees 7:28). So God must have been behind that Big Bang.

Now, I'm rather taking it for granted that you do believe in

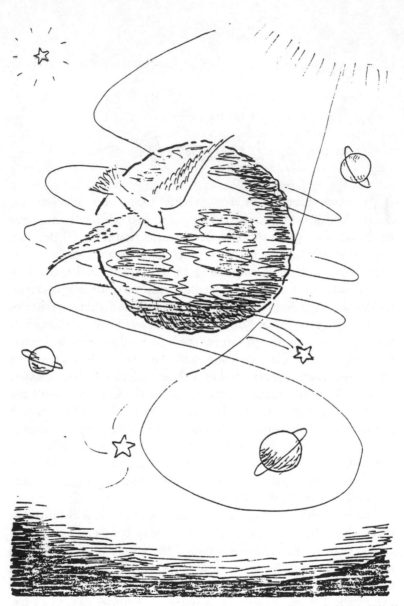

As Creation took shape, and stars, planets and star-dust of all kinds fell into the places God had assigned for them, the Spirit of God hovered over the handiwork of the Word uttered by the Godhead, and our world came into being. This world of men and women that "God so loved that he would give his only Son that all might have eternal life"

14

God. Perhaps you don't, or you're not sure. Well, what if there is no God? It would take a powerful lot of explaining to convince me that a Big Bang came all by itself. A Bang big enough to start off all the marvels of our earth and all the universe. A Bang powerful enough to give birth to energy such as is produced by steam, gas, electricity and, for far greater reason, by nuclear reaction. A Bang packed with enough intelligence to pass on, even to ordinary folk like you and me, let alone geniuses of one sort or another. A Bang that could set hearts ticking and pulsing, not only with life blood but with Love. All that without a Big, Powerful, Intelligent, Living and Loving Being behind it. My word, it would take a lot of explaining! I like my answer best.

This is my answer: God spoke, and when God spoke the impact of the Almighty Word of God, breaking upon the immensity of nothingness would have been gigantic, more than sufficient to cause the biggest of Big Bangs. God spoke and the divine Mighty Word leapt forth and creation began. As the little boy, learning about the creation, asked, "But where did God get the bits?" Ah! That's a good question because, of course, there weren't any bits.

God just spoke and God's Word isn't like any other word. God's Word is an expression of Godself and, as God can't be divided, the expression of Godself, God's Word, is Godself. There is only one God but there are three divine persons in God. All distinct, all equal, all God but one and the same God, only one God. The second person is often referred to as the "Word of God", and this is who we are talking about now. God spoke and, "The Word was God. He was with God in the beginning. Through him all things came to be. Not one thing had its being but through him" (John 1:1–3).

So, when God spoke the immense nothingness of empty space was filled with the projection of Godself – The Word of God. Now, we have to be careful. I am using human language which is terribly limited and inadequate when we are talking about God. God is indescribable. We do not understand God

15

one bit, so it is ever so easy to be misleading. I would ask the reader not to jump to conclusions and misinterpret my words. If I say that creation was a projection of the Godhead I am not saying that the universe, or nature, or creation, is a form of God. That would be pantheism (identification of God with the universe) which is not at all correct. I am trying to emphasize that it was God, and God alone who was involved in, responsible for, creation, and therefore everything created in some way reflects something of God, and God's continual presence pervades everything created and keeps it in being, and still does, and that includes you and me. So no one, absolutely no one can afford to say, "I'm not interested in religion. I can get along very well without God." That would make no more sense than saying, "I'm not interested in breathing. I can get along very well without air."

So, remembering that this is only limited human language, one could almost say that matter was in some sort a crystallization of the Word of God, the Word that was Godself, shattering into myriads of particles of all sizes and shapes, "stardust" we might call it, all sent spinning and whirling out in every direction, millions and millions of miles into nothingness, "space" we usually call it now.

Creation had begun but it certainly hadn't finished, it still hasn't done that. Somehow, through a long period of evolution (which scientists know a lot more about than I do), parts of this crystallized Word of God became the universe we know: the sun, the moon and the stars, and all that is upon the earth, the plants, the creeping creatures of all kinds, the big animals and beasts, and human beings, "Remember man that thou art dust" (Genesis 3:19). Ah yes! but stardust, God's glorious stardust. Do you see it? We are not isolated units for we are all part of a whole. This is very important for our destinies. Though seemingly so different, we are all bound up with the destiny of the whole. No one and nothing is left out.

When God's utterance filled the nothingness of space with myriads of morsels of stardust it was certainly not a capricious act, not a "There it goes, let's see what happens next!" kind of gesture. No, God does not work like that. In the Book of Proverbs we read: "Yahweh created me *when his purpose unfolded* before the oldest of his works. From everlasting I was firmly set" (Proverbs 8:22).

So God had a purpose that unfolded under the guidance of Wisdom, "the master craftsman" (Proverbs 8:30). "By Wisdom, Yahweh set the Earth on its foundations, by discernment he fixed the heavens firm. Through his knowledge the depths were carved out and the clouds rain down the dew" (Proverbs 3:19–20). This unfolding will continue until the plan and purpose of God is fulfilled: "The Word that goes forth from my mouth does not return to me empty, without carrying out my will and succeeding in what it was sent to do" (Isaiah 55:11).

CHAPTER FIVE

The Time Machine

There was one kind of book I really enjoyed reading when I was a youngster. It was that in which kids had adventures visiting other ages in time by some kind of magic means. I remember there was one in which the children had a carpet which they could sit on and be carried back to the time of, say, Robin Hood, or the Druids. In another, a magic ring, which they rubbed, fulfilled the same function. And there were others. H. G. Wells brought the notion up to adult level with his more sophisticated "Time Machine", but the idea was the same. Not content with being where and when we are in reality, we want to know what it was, or will be, like at some other time and somewhere else. This has an enormous fascination for people. We, ourselves, in ordinary life, are limited by time. We can't go back and we can't go forward. We are restricted and we like to break out, even if it's only in imagination, and be free of the ties of time. God is free like that. God is timeless. God is Lord of Time. I suppose, subconsciously, we want to emulate God. It's the old temptation: "You will be like Gods" (Genesis 3:5). Well, does all this mean that there was never a time before God was?

Now, that last question is asked all the wrong way. It talks about "Time" and uses the past tense "God *was*". We can't say God "Was" but only, God "*is*". God is the "Eternal Present". Of course, I can't really explain this. The only thing that I can do is to tell you about an image that I have that gives me just an inkling as to how it is. Hopefully it will mean something to you too.

Think of an enormous hollow globe. In the centre of this

globe there is a powerful lamp. This lamp radiates light in every direction, lighting up the interior surface of the globe. You can't say that any part of the globe is illuminated sooner or later than any other part because, obviously, every part of the globe receives the light at the same time. The shiny inside of the globe reflects the light back from all parts equally simultaneously. It all happens together.

Now turn off the light and look at the outside of the globe. Hold a candle to it. A small part of the outer surface is lit up. The rest is in shadow. The candle is moved right round the globe's surface, as it travels different parts are illuminated one after the other, but the rest is in darkness. In time the whole surface has been lit up, but not all at once. It takes time for the light to go from place to place all over the globe. The lighting up takes place progressively. It didn't take time for the central lamp to light up the inside of the globe all at once. The lamp is not bound by time. The candle is bound by time.

God is at the centre of everything, timewise as well as placewise. Therefore everything is present to God at once. God is the Eternal Present.

Let's look at all that very carefully. We have the tendency to think of eternity in terms of time. We think of it as a very, very, very long time whether we are looking ahead or back. We might illustrate our thinking something like this:

| past-eternity | now | future-eternity |

$$\longleftarrow \mathrel{\Big|} \longrightarrow$$

and we wonder where the arrows point to and how far we'd have to go to get there, how long it would take, and what we'd find when we got there. That's the way our minds work because we are time-conditioned and time-bound, and time works like that. Eternity doesn't work like that. Eternity has rules of its own. As I have already tried to demonstrate with my theory-story of a globe, it works more like this, I think:

everywhere, everytime all at once, *now* all the time. Even if you try to find the beginning or end of the outer circle, you can't. You just go round and round and round all the time, whichever way you go, and, you never get farther away from the centre of the circle either. If then, God always *is*, we can't say that God either started to be or will cease being. That's what we mean when we say that God is eternal.

Similarly, if God always *is* we can't say God "created". We can only say God "creates", so there never was or will be a time when God is not "creating". God is always uttering the divine Word so the Word of God is also eternal. Questions like, "Why did God wait so long before creating the world?" or, "What did God do before creating the world?" lose their sense and don't have any meaning at all. God never has to wait. It's always now for God. It's always happening. But as one of the things that God creates is "time" and time is not eternal, we can't say that creation is eternal. That certainly is a problem.

In fact, I know that my globe theory doesn't answer this or all our other questions, but it does allow for the possibility of there being two different ways of functioning, or being: the time-function, illustrated by the candle which is small and limited and advances progressively, and the lamp-function which has no progression but just "shines" everywhere all the time.

God doesn't have to wait for anything. We have to wait to understand eternity. We have to wait until we have been transformed and our limitations have all been left behind and we see God "face to face. The knowledge that I have now is imperfect; but then I shall know as fully as I am known"

(1 Corinthians 13:12). In the meantime St Peter, quoting from Psalm 90, reminds us that "with the Lord 'a day' can mean a thousand years, and a thousand years is like a day" (2 Peter 3:8).

We find all this very hard to grasp. Waiting seems long. We get impatient. We are in a hurry. We say things like, "Why doesn't God do this? or that? or put this or that right?" We speak like that because we just can't understand that, as God *is*, there is never any question of God's being in a hurry. God never has to calculate what has to be done and God never changes. Neither can anyone ever get the better of God. How could they, since God is the Lord of time whereas everyone else is bound by it. Traumatic dramas seem to be enacted as time goes on, as time goes by in our little world, but the outcome already *is* to God. God's control and God's triumph are perfectly assured because God always *is*. We can't understand. Let us at least accept. If we can do that the problem doesn't bother us.

I am insisting upon all this because it has some very important implications, particularly when we come to ask questions about the person of Jesus, what he means to us today and if he meant anything at all to those people who lived in the thousands of centuries before his birth just 2,000 years ago. As I am timebound I can only deal with one thing at a time, so I will talk about Jesus's place in time and in eternity when I get to that chapter.

In the meanwhile I would suggest that it is best not to probe too deeply into this mystery of eternity, for mystery it is and we will only be tying ourselves into knots. In any case there are so many things we don't understand. At least for my part I know there are many things I don't understand such as computers, microchips and many more. But I know there are other people who do understand them and I am quite content to leave the understanding to them, so that's all right. Those people are cleverer and more knowledgeable than I am. For far greater reason I can say that God is cleverer and more knowledgeable than I am (it would be a very puny God who weren't). I am quite content that God should be all wise and all knowing. In fact I need that for my security. My answer to all that is Faith, and Faith itself is a gift of God. If we haven't got much Faith let's ask God to give us a little more, and remain at Peace.

CHAPTER SIX

Christkind

A stone, a flower a butterfly; the rolling hills, the flocks of sheep and girls and boys at play; those dark grey clouds and pouring rain, those cats and dogs, those bustling crowds in busy streets; whatever is creation all about? What does it mean?

The mighty Word came forth from God and creation was begun. All that was made was made by God, God's Word, and for the Word the world was made. All nature with the magnificence of its mountains, rivers and seas, all birds and beasts and creeping insects, and, crowning all this glory, humankind. What higher things could God create? Surely with humankind creation reached perfection! But wait. "Greater things than this you shall see."

Not humankind but Jesus Christ, the Word made man, would bring creation to perfection. "In him were created all things in heaven and on earth . . . and all things were created through him and for him . . . *he held all things in unity*" (Colossians 1:16–18), ". . . him who fills the whole creation" (Ephesians 1:23). All creation, then, somehow finds its place in the Word, all creation is in the Word and the Word fills all creation. To bring creation to perfection the Word entered creation in an even closer way. The Word took human nature uniting God and man in the person of Jesus Christ. In doing so the Word not only became a man but took on all humanity. This was the plan of God so that men and women would not just be humankind but would be raised to an infinitely higher level, they would be Christkind, sharing with Jesus his affiliation with God – that is to say they would have sonship and daughtership of God, kinship with Christ, they would be of his kind,

23

What is creation? A Word of God uttered into the immensity of nothingness. And God, the God of love, God who is Love, so loved this Word spoken from all eternity, that into this created world "God sent his only Son" and the Word became man, the man Jesus. Jesus is in the world and "his fullness fills the whole creation" as he draws all humankind unto himself so that all may have eternal life

Christkind. This would be possible only if they shared his nature and the Word's nature is divine. Of this divine nature God planned to give humanity a share; that would not make them Gods, no, they would retain their own identity but would henceforth be so to speak, of the family of God.

When this was achieved the Word would return to God, not empty, but bearing humanity into the realm of God. This we call "eternal life". "The Word that goes forth from my mouth does not return to me empty, without carrying out my will and succeeding in what it was sent to do" (Isaiah 55:11).

This was God's plan and so staggering it is that we need to pray earnestly and reflect deeply so as to bring home to ourselves something of its meaning.

This was God's plan but, to be fit in some degree for this high elevation, humanity had to be not only beautiful and intelligent but also free. There was nothing wanting in God's handiwork. Humanity is beautiful, intelligent and also free. Free to accept the gift of divine adoption, receiving a share in the divine life itself, and free to reject it. No one could possibly be so closely united to God unwillingly. That would be unworthy, certainly, of God, but also of God's masterpiece, humanity. So from the first appearance of human beings upon this earth, this choice was given them: accept God's sovereignty and receive eternal life or – well, what is the opposite of life? Death. The account of this requirement of accepting God's sovereignty is presented to us in symbolical form in Genesis: "Then Yahweh (God) gave the man this admonition, 'You may eat indeed of all the trees in the garden. Nevertheless of the tree of the knowledge of good and evil you are not to eat, for on the day you eat of it you shall most surely die'" (Genesis 2:17).

What exactly happened in those far-off days we don't know. No journalist or cameraman was there to report it. Legends and myths grew up around the story and we know that humanity made the wrong choice, chose to go it alone without God, thinking that somehow in this way men and women would be "like to God" (Genesis 3:5).

The effects of this choice were, and still are, disastrous. Human beings were thrown back on their own resources which, without God, are totally inadequate. Humanity made a mess of things. But God's plans were not to be thwarted. No one can thwart God's plans. God would not be God if that were possible. The wrong choice was there, it had to be reversed, rectified, cancelled in some way so that humanity could once more be reconciled to God. Humanity was not able to do this. God came to their aid. When the Word came into the world and was united to humanity by taking human nature in the womb of Mary and being born as a human child, this child, Jesus, came as a saviour, a redeemer. In a tremendous act of sacrifice he gave his human life back to God. This sacrifice was a total recognition of God's sovereignty. That is the meaning of all sacrifice but this sacrifice, being offered by a man who was also God had infinite value and power. Power to reconcile man to God. Reconciliation was achieved and humanity could once more be affiliated to God as sons and daughters, heirs to the heavenly homeland.

Humanity, yes, but each single member of our race still is free to make his or her own personal choice, to accept reconciliation with God or to go it his or her own way. How this works out in the life of each one of us, how we can rise from humankind to Christkind, how we can lose this gift again and what we must do then, all this and much more will fill the pages of this book as we find out more about Jesus Christ and what becoming Christkind means.

CHAPTER SEVEN

Fill my House unto the Fullest

(My chapter title is taken from "Fill my house unto the fullest", *20th Century Folk Hymnal*, Vol. 2, Peter Kearney, Kevin Mayhew Limited.)

Many villages can boast an old church. Some of them are hundreds of years old and very picturesque. Artists and photographers seem to be drawn to these old churches and can often be seen painting or taking photos of the old buildings, and beautiful pictures they make.

One of the oldest churches that I have visited was nearly one thousand years old. There are a few churches even older than that, and as for ruins of churches, well, they go back even more hundreds of years. This is true, not only of Britain but in many parts of the world, especially in the Middle East, which, after all, was the cradle of Christianity. This tells us something. It tells us that people have been gathering together to worship ever since Christianity began. That is why the Greek word for church is "Ekklesia", which means "assembly".

It's good to look at the meaning of the words we use so as to really know what we are talking about. The English word "church" comes originally from another Greek word "kuriakon" meaning "the Lord's house", from "kurios", "lord" (Concise Oxford Dictionary).

When we talk about "church" we may be referring to an actual building or we may be speaking about something much deeper. Some people think of "the Church" as an association or society of people who believe the same thing and worship in the same way. They often think of their society being ruled or governed by the clergy. Some think that it is the clergy – the Pope, the bishops and the priests who are the Church. The rest of us are called the laity who used to be thought of almost as an audience, congregation if you like, but hardly "the Church". That, of course is quite wrong, we are all "the Church", equally the Church though we have different roles in it. It is also wrong, and completely missing the point, to think of the Church just as a society or association, just as wrong as to think that the Church is only the building that the artist is painting. What then is the Church?

St Paul says that Christ is "the Head of the Church, *which is his body*, the *fullness of him who fills the whole creation*" (Ephesians 1:23). Can we take that in? The Church is the "Fullness" of Christ, or the "Body" of Christ. "Body" and "fullness" are important words to dwell upon here.

Jesus took his human body from Mary and was a man like any other. After his resurrection he had a glorified body (which we will talk about in Chapter Thirteen). When we talk about the Church as being Christ's body we are obviously not meaning his human body. Christ is not limited to his human body. When Jesus said, "I will draw all things to myself", he meant he would unite us to himself, sharing his divine life with us. He identifies us with himself. One way of expressing this is to say that we are the extension of Christ. The word "fullness" expresses this meaning rather well. And this is the Church.

This is difficult to understand. It is indeed! This is the "mystery, the hidden plan he (God) so kindly made in Christ from the beginning . . . that he would bring *everything together under Christ as the head*" (Ephesians 1:9–10).

So, all those who become so much one with Christ that they are not only humankind but Christkind are "the Church". This is something elevated, holy and spiritual and so has nothing to do with being merely members of any human society. Human society, however, there appears to be. Of course, when you are dealing with human beings you have to have human functioning and structures and, I might add, human behaviour and scandals

28

too. But the human side of the Church is only the visible garment of the spiritual reality of our oneness with Christ. So the Church that we are talking about is not just the House of the Lord but the Body, or Fullness of the Lord. This makes membership of this Church-which-is-Christ of the utmost importance.

Jesus sometimes spoke of a "Kingdom" and stressed God's desire for everyone to enter it. He spoke of a king inviting guests to a wedding banquet (Matthew 22:1). Marriage is a union in which two become one. In Jesus's wedding banquet many become one, sharing Christ's life and sonship of God. In Jesus's story many of the guests didn't want to go to the wedding, so the king sent servants out into the highways and byways to collect up everyone they could find, so anxious was the king that his wedding feast be full.

This kingdom that Jesus spoke about is not only the Church which we know on earth but also the eternal kingdom of Heaven, where, at one with the Word, we are meant to be part of the love life of the Trinity. "If we are children we are heirs as well: heirs of God and coheirs with Christ" (Romans 8:17) – heirs to the Kingdom.

In Part III of this book we will examine a little more closely this invitation but, first of all, in Part II, we will take a longer look at Jesus, the Word of God in his manhood.

Part II: *God's Word on Earth*

"The Virgin shall conceive and give birth to a son and you will call him Emmanuel . . . a name which means 'God-is-with-us'" (Matthew 1:23 quoting Isaiah 7:14).

Jesus is this "Emmanuel". He is God and he is among us. He is the beginning, the centre and the end of God's plan but do we *know* him? Do we *know* this Jesus who, although he was the Word of God, Godself, was also a real, true man sharing completely our human condition? This Jesus who finally died a real death for our salvation: "Since all the children share the same blood and flesh, he too shared equally in it so that by his death he could take away all the power of the Devil, who had power over death" (Hebrews 2:14).

The Word of God entered humankind as any other human being: born of a mother, developing, growing, learning, gaining experience, living and finally dying. The humanity of Jesus did not cancel out his divinity, neither did the fact that he was truly God prevent him from being a real man. He came with a mission and he was guided by the Spirit in the fulfilment of his mission. By his death he defeated evil, and when God raised him to life again he entered the glorified state of eternity, not only on his own account, but as a pledge of our being given hope of following him into his eternal glory.

In Part II we will be looking at some aspects of Jesus's human life and mission and what it must have meant to him as a man, as to us and to all humanity.

CHAPTER EIGHT

Paving the Way

Take a peep into the maternity room in one of our big hospitals. That is, if they will let you in. All the latest technology has been brought into play to ensure the purest cleanliness. Not a grain of dust that could harbour a microbe is allowed to settle in this sanctuary of sterilized cleanliness: sterilized towels, white coats etc. are all the rigour, and precautions of all kinds are taken to ensure that no infection meets the newly-born infant on his or her arrival into this world. And back at home there is a cot with soft sheets and woollen blankets, a pram, dainty little garments and much more besides, all lovingly prepared for the impatiently awaited small VIP who will soon be the centre and hub of the family circle.

And what of the Son of God? He who was not just the centre of a family circle but the hub of the whole universe as well as being its beginning and its end. What preparations were made for his coming, what precautions were taken at the beginning of his human life? He was born in a primitive, and probably rather dirty, cowshed! Ah yes, but there is a spotlessness which is higher and more important than mere material cleanliness, and there are gifts more precious than any of the manufactured articles that parents usually prepare for the arrival of their child.

The Holy Spirit it was who saw to the preparations for the coming into this world of the Lord of Lords as a human child. The Spirit was not concerned with an antiseptic maternity ward, or anything of that kind, but a mother was prepared, a mother who was immaculate.

Long before the birth of Jesus, the Spirit hovered over Mary even before she herself was conceived. The role of the Spirit at that moment was to protect her from all that contaminating smog that clogs up our spiritual health (see Chapter 15). That smog we call sin. Mary was to become the sanctuary where the divine "seed" was to flower, so right and fitting it was that no smog was ever permitted to pollute her soul, not even from the very first instant. That is what we mean when we speak of the "Immaculate Conception". Those may be big words but the meaning is quite simple – protected from original sin from the very start. "She is a breath of the power of God, pure emanation of the glory of the Almighty: hence nothing impure can find a way into her. She is a reflection of the eternal light, untarnished mirror of God's active power, image of his goodness" (Wisdom 7:25–26).

Someone may say at this point: "You mean the Virgin Birth, don't you?" No, I don't. That is something quite different. We mustn't mix up the two births, Mary's own and that of Jesus. The "Immaculate Conception" refers to the beginning of Mary's life. The "Virgin Birth" is about the way she conceived Jesus. Her Immaculate Conception was in view of her becoming the Mother of God.

Mary was protected from sin so that everything would be spotless for the conception of her own son, Jesus, because that conception was very, very special and quite different from all others. This was when the Word of God leaped down into Mary's womb without the intervention of a human father to initiate his conception. Mary was a virgin and she conceived Jesus, not in the human way, but by the leaping down of the Word, overshadowed by the Holy Spirit.

But, when all is said and done, who exactly is this Mary who was so signally picked out? Well, to start with she was just a young girl who lived, nearly 2,000 years ago, in a village called Nazareth, in Galilee. Nazareth still exists in spite of that length of time. It is in modern Israel. We are not told anything definite about her family, only there is a tradition that her mother was called Anne and her father Joachim. We are told, however, that she was engaged to a man named Joseph who was a carpenter or joiner. You see, just ordinary people, like most of us, expecting to lead just ordinary lives. But God had plans. The Word of God was to take that mighty leap down, right into humanity, and so be born as a baby. A mother had to be part of that plan. God chose Mary to be that mother.

This choice was all part of the eternal divine plan, so Mary's role, Mary herself, was present in the mind of God in a special way when that first creative Word shattered the emptiness of uncreated nothingness. So in some sense she was present when creation began. This presence was not like the pre-existence of Jesus, he was the Word and the Word was always existent. No, her presence was like a reflection of his, a foreshadowing rather than an existence, but nevertheless it gave Mary a prophetic presence and influence in the world from its very beginning.

We catch our first glimpse of this in Genesis 3, where God, speaking to the serpent (Spirit or Evil), warns it that the woman (Mary) would be its enemy and her "seed" (Jesus) would crush its head – Jesus, son of Mary would overcome Satan, that wholly evil spirit.

Then again we sense the presence of Mary in the feminine figure, "Wisdom" in the Book of Proverbs. Wisdom is an attribute of God. The Word of God is often referred to as "Divine Wisdom", but personified Wisdom, of the Scriptures, was a feminine figure. There seems to be a beautiful fusion here of Jesus and Mary, "Wisdom" seems to represent them both. Of course all femininity comes from God, as does also all masculinity. All creation reflects the Godhead. God didn't have any pieces, outside of Godself, to make the world with! But God infused into Mary the eternal femininity of the divinity in its purest form, and her perfume preceded her elusively under the guise of Wisdom of the Scriptures. She was also predicted under various other Biblical types. Surely it was of Mary, rather than of Judith, that the following praises were sung: "You are the glory of Jerusalem! You are the great pride of Israel! You are the highest honour of our race!" (Judith 15:10).

The highest honour Mary certainly received when she was

chosen to be the mother of the Word of God, that is, Mother of God. She might have been an ordinary young girl but there was nothing ordinary about her calling. And that calling to be the Word's own mother was the meaning of everything about her. There would have been no foreshadowing, no immaculate conception, no virgin birth without it. Neither would Mary later have been assumed body and soul into heaven. Nor would she have meant anything special to us.

As it is, she means everything. For it was she who gave us Jesus, and in becoming mother of him who is the beginning, the end and the centre of all creation, and of humanity in particular, she also became, in a very real sense, mother of all humanity. Through Jesus we become children of God, his own brothers and sisters – even closer, one with him, hence children of his mother, Mary. Through her we are born to supernatural life because she became the mother of that very life that is the life of our souls.

She is certainly the "highest honour of our race", not only the most loving and the most faithful but the strongest and bravest woman the human race has ever produced. People often speak of the divine motherhood as the great privilege of Mary, but it is easy to forget the other side of it. Great and very great privilege it undoubtedly was, greater than we can appreciate or understand, but it also demanded an enormous amount of stretching on the part of a creature to measure up to it and she must often have felt utterly devastated. But there was never any word of her chickening out, not even when her motherhood led her to stand at the foot of the Cross watching the agony and death of her Son.

Measure up to it she couldn't, not on her own, so God came to her aid. The Holy Spirit overshadowed her, but that in no way took away her merit. By the power of her divine motherhood she is given the strength to bridge the gap between Heaven and Earth and in so doing she seconds the priestly bridgehood of her son (see Chapter 10).

That divine son came to gather all humanity to himself, and

through him to Godself. So Mary in becoming his mother became our mother also. Every child that is conceived is a child of God, destined to be eternally united to Christ in the Trinity. Every child then is potentially Christ. Every child is holy.

CHAPTER NINE

Pathfinding

A friend of mine was once invited to a school Nativity Play. This was many years ago when there was more Christianity in Britain than there is now and everybody, or nearly everybody had at least some idea as to what Christmas was about and who the persons in the Nativity story were.

My friend came home quite upset, shocked even. At the height of the performance, when Mary was seated at centre stage, holding the Infant Jesus in her arms, surrounded by worshipping shepherds and kings, a small boy sitting in the row behind my friend, suddenly piped up: "'Oo's the kid?" Babies he understood, but all this bowing and kneeling must have meant that the "kid" was someone special, but who?

"'Oo's the kid?" The question was crude but, put into other words it is one that we often find very difficult to answer. Yes, we usually admit that Jesus was God. We often find it more difficult to grasp the reality of his manhood. Ever since the beginning of Christianity people have been wondering, speculating and arguing about Jesus and how far he was God and how far he was man. I'm not writing a book of apologetics so I won't go into the arguments or proofs used by different people, I just accept the basic Christian teaching that he was *fully* God and *fully* man. However having accepted that, it is extremely interesting and useful to look at him as man and wonder at what point and to what extent the man Jesus understood his divinity.

He certainly did realize it and said so clearly: "The Father and I are one" (John 10:30), but at what stage in his life he came to the full realization of this is not clearly revealed. The question is still open to discussion provided no doubt is thrown upon his Godhead.

It is quite obvious that as a baby he didn't know. Infants' awareness of themselves is a growing, an unfolding thing. This was surely the case with Jesus too, as he was a normal baby. He must have been a very intelligent child; the ability with which he dealt with his hecklers later in life was proof enough of his intelligence. He must also have been a very prayerful child; his habit of spending long nights in prayer as a man didn't develop overnight, so the Father spoke to him as God to man and taught him (as man) many things. Then there was his mother. It is difficult to believe that, at some point or other, she did not tell him the circumstances of his birth. It was probably she who first introduced him to the Scriptures which he must also have learnt in the synagogue and in whatever synagogue-school he attended. He must have gone to school as he could read. The Hebrews always set great store on literacy.

Like every Jewish boy, when Jesus was twelve years of age he became "bar mitzvah", that is "a son of the Law". This meant that he had reached religious adult status and was able to assume the responsibilities and obligations of every adult Israelite; responsibilities and obligations to which his parents had committed him at his circumcision. (A bit like Christian parents making promises in the name of their child at baptism.) One of these Jewish obligations was a pilgrimage to Jerusalem for the feast of the Passover.

For the lad, Jesus, this was a golden opportunity. His self-awareness had been steadily growing, fed no doubt by his reading of the Scriptures. He probably had a shrewd idea as to his identity but needed confirmation. Where better could he get this than from the appointed guardians of the Scriptures, the priests and doctors of the Law? "They found him in the Temple, sitting among the doctors, *listening* to them and *asking them questions.*" They, obviously struck by his precociousness, quizzed him and "all those who heard him were astounded at his intelligence and his replies" (Luke 2:46–7).

I can make a guess that Jesus was querying the doctors about the Messianic prophecies, some of which were rather obscure, and it would have been interesting to have been a fly on the wall during those three days of talks and discussions that Jesus had with the doctors in the Temple! Failing that I combed the Scriptures for these prophecies presuming that Jesus was familiar with them. I can make no guess what comments the doctors made on them but it is quite plain that Jesus came out of the experience confirmed in what must have already been a growing realization of his unique identity of Son of God – one of the divine persons of the Trinity – Godself. This would have been so momentous for him that it was no wonder that it totally absorbed him for three days. He probably didn't even notice that Mary and Joseph had left without him. When they came back and found him, so full was he of the knowledge that he now possessed that he couldn't understand that they didn't know too. God was in a unique way his Father and that he himself had a mission: "Did you not know that I must be about my Father's affairs?" (Luke 2:49).

Whether he knew or not exactly what that mission was, or would entail, is not clear. He did know, however, from the prophecies that "the one who was to come" (Matthew 11:2) was foretold under many guises: king, prophet, priest, saviour, shepherd, son of man, servant. He would be royal and victorious, he would champion the poor and oppressed, he would establish a new covenant and he would bear our sufferings and sorrows. There was certainly much that he still needed to reflect upon, pray through and seek enlightenment from the Father about. But he was sure now who his father was and that the "Spirit was upon him". This study and preparation for his mission was to be continued for another eighteen years.

However, before actually starting to teach, Jesus had a dramatic experience when he was baptized by John. This must have been not only a dramatic experience, but, for Jesus, as man, it could only have been traumatic. He, man in time, formally and publicly accepted as his own, the role of the eternal Word of God, who he also was, leaping down into our condition. He accepted the role and the consequences, and heard the Father ratify his identity and actions.

What it must mean for a man to be at the same time God is something completely outside our understanding. We can only stand back and wonder. His divinity was always there. Was it, perhaps, hidden in his subconscious allowing his humanity to act like an ordinary man? Did his human soul have an awareness of his divinity at times of deep prayer? I do not know, neither does anyone else, but surely, living up to the total, timeless mission of the Word of God, must have stretched and strained to the utmost every human fibre in this real man, Jesus of Nazareth. The climax was to come at Gethsemane and Calvary, perhaps relief only came with the Resurrection, but now I am jumping ahead too fast. The demands on his humanity were certainly very, very great, and pondering this makes us realize our enormous debt to him, even just as man.

In the meantime the Spirit of God, the Holy Spirit, was given to his manhood to help, guide and strengthen him. After the event of his baptism the Spirit led him out into the wilderness for forty days – "to be tempted by the Devil" (Matthew 4:1).

This was the Adversary, the Accuser of mankind. Jesus was to defeat him for the salvation of all of us. How could he do this if he never encountered him? Encounter him he did and sent him packing. Then, weakened in body but strengthened in soul after his forty days' fast, he set out on his mission. He had found his path without possibility of doubt and would walk it to the end. Returning to Nazareth, his home town, he read in the synagogue from the Prophet Isaiah: "The Spirit of the Lord has been given to me, for he has anointed me. He has sent me to bring the good news to the poor, to proclaim liberty to captives and to the blind new sight, to set the downtrodden free, to proclaim the Lord's year of favour." (Luke 4:18).

What all that means in the life of each one of us unfolds gradually as, under the guidance of the Holy Spirit, we also seek our own pathways into our oneness with Christ.

In this chapter the accent has been all on the manhood of Jesus. This is important for our understanding of his closeness to us and his loving compassion for us. But we must never let this obscure his divinity. That would be completely missing the point. It is Jesus, in his humanity, who discloses and manifests for us the divinity, the Father-God.

This man Jesus, we must never forget was, no, *is*, the eternal Word of God, present in the world from the very beginning of creation. "Before Abraham was, I am" Jesus himself declared (John 8:58), and he will be with us "until the end of time" (Matthew 28:20). Jesus, the epitome of the Godhead in man, Jesus the high point of Creation; Jesus who draws all things to himself so that all creation is in him united to the Godhead. Jesus – Creation!

The most terrible thing that could happen to anyone of us would be to take the wrong road, resist that divine "draw" and to fail to be united to Christ in the Godhead.

CHAPTER TEN

Bridges

Many years ago I was invited to spend the day with some Girl Guides who were camping in the mountains not far from my house. They were making their camp around the theme of "bridges" and they asked me to talk at the camp fire about "bridges". I remember saying that, as I had been a guide many, many years earlier, I was myself a kind of bridge between their generation and mine. I went on to talk about the way we could be bridges between people but I don't remember any details of my little talk. Thinking about it now I have come up with a number of things I might have said and possibly did say.

First of all a bridge is a link. It joins two separate sites. There are places that could be connected by other means, for example fording a stream or swimming a river. Other gaps are so wide that only a bridge can span them. These "gaps" might be situations, relationships bedevilled by misunderstandings, long-term alienation, differences of race, creed, colour or culture etc. and only a third party could make a bridge.

A bridge links two separate positions and permits traffic to pass between the two. It is the bridge that bears the weight of that traffic whichever way it may be travelling. It must be strong to carry that strain! That is what bridges are for, so they are fulfilled in the accomplishment of that purpose. When you come to think of it a bridge is very "selfless"; it exists for others. It serves, it is a servant. A bridge makes no noise but it hears all the noise of the traffic that passes over it. It listens.

I haven't been able to find any reference to bridges in the Bible. I suppose there was not much engineering in those days, people seemed to ford any streams that they had to cross. The

No one can draw a picture of Spirit, no one can draw God. We can merely use symbols that speak to us of God. God is everywhere in heaven and on earth. There is no distance for God. The lightning that flashes across the heavens or rips the sky apart is but a feeble image of the Word of God who, at a moment in time, "leapt into the heart" of creation, into "that doomed land" so needing a Saviour for having turned away from the Word of its Creator. "God so loved the world that he gave his only Son so that everyone who believes in him may not be lost but may have eternal life" (John 3:16)

nearest thing to a bridge was supplied by Godself. It was a ladder. A ladder does bridge a distance between two places and the significant thing is that the two are not on the same level, one is much higher than the other. This was the case with God's ladder, though we usually called it "Jacob's ladder". Jacob was on a journey and he stopped at nightfall and slept out in the open just where he was. "He had a dream; a ladder was there, standing on the ground with its top reaching to Heaven. . . . Yahweh was there, standing over him, saying: 'I am Yahweh . . . I will give to you and your descendants the land on which you are lying' . . . Jacob awoke from his sleep and said: 'Truly Yahweh is in this place and I never knew it! This is nothing less than a house of God; this is the gate of Heaven!'" (Genesis 28:13–17).

Yahweh promised to give Jacob and his descendants a land. This was the Promised Land which the Hebrews were heading for in Exodus, and which we understand as being symbolical of Heaven, or eternal life with the Trinity. Like Jacob, we are only too often unaware of the presence of God and that wherever we are is the House of God, we are totally unaware of how great are the promises made to us. We don't realize that the Gate of Heaven is open quite close to us with a ladder leading up to it with "angels of God going up it and coming down" (Genesis 28:12). In other words communication between ourselves and God is always possible.

Here, however, we have a problem. We are creatures of this world, that is our natural habitat, where we belong and feel at home. God, the Trinity, is way out of our sphere and yet is inviting us into the life of the Trinity, in fact God made us with that in mind. The problem is, how do we bridge the gap? How can we humans hoist ourselves up to God's heights? We can't. But God can do it for us. God has done so. God has built us a bridge. This bridge obviously must have ends in both spheres. The Word of God became man, Jesus, God and man, and he alone, can bridge the gap between human beings and the Godhead. He is our "Jacob's Ladder" that spans the gulf. But a bridge is really wasted if no one crosses it. That is just what we have to do and we do it when we accept to be united to him in his Church-Body.

This is such a tremendous, breathtaking notion that God knew that men and women couldn't take it in without a lot of preparation. This preparation was, to a great extent, what the Old Testament was all about. In it we find prophets foretelling the coming of the Messiah, the Christ, (the Bridge), and prophetical figures foreshadowing the "greater things that you will see" that were to come. Jacob's ladder is one example of this. Moses was another.

Moses was a go-between for the people in their relationship with God. The People were so impressed by the almighty power and grandeur of God that they were afraid. "Speak to us yourself," they said to Moses, "and we will listen, but do not let God speak to us, or we shall die." Moses answered: "Do not be afraid" (Exodus 20:19–20). Moses acted as the bridge between the people and God.

Possibly up to the time of the Exodus the rank and file of the Hebrews had only a very vague notion of the Godhead, about four hundred years of oppression under an alien people and surrounded by the worship of false Gods would account for that. Very often we are not much better but sometimes our own indifference is the cause. However, by the time of Moses the Hebrews had come to know God but not well enough not to be afraid. Mind you, there are two kinds of fear of God, one good and one bad. If people are afraid because they think that God is hard, cruel or callous, doesn't care about them or is ruthless or takes pleasure in seeing them suffer or anything like that, then that is a bad kind of fear based on an idolatrous notion of God. We have no reason to fear a God who is Love and Mercy, plans eternal happiness for us and even becomes man to build a bridge between the Godhead and human creatures.

But when we consider the distance between ourselves and God, our creaturehood before God the Creator, we would be bold, in the worst sense of the word, not to stand in awe and respect of God. This is the fear that is "the beginning of wisdom" (Proverbs 9:10) which makes us willing to sacrifice all rather than risk losing union with God. It makes us doubt our own wisdom and strength to obtain it, and therefore makes us cry out to God, "Make sure I do not follow pernicious ways, and guide me in the way that is everlasting" (Psalm 139 (138):24).

I used the word "sacrifice" just now. Sacrifice played a great part in the act of mediation – or "bridge-building" – between the people of God and Yahweh. The offering of sacrifice was one of the principal functions of the priests who were appointed to the role of "go-between" in the relationship between the People and God. It was a two-way role: the priests presented the gifts and the prayers of the people to God, and also responded in God's name by blessing the people. As we saw in Jacob's dream, the angels were ascending and descending.

These priests were bridges between creatures and the Creator. But the old Hebrew priesthood was fragile. The priests were human beings like the rest of the people, even the High Priest who, alone, had the right to enter the Holy of Holies where God's presence was especially situated, was a man subject to human weakness and death itself. These weak "bridges" couldn't "carry the weight". Something else was needed.

All these foreshadowings: Jacob's ladder, Moses, the Hebrew priesthood, were leading men and women to the idea of mediation, bridge-building, between God and ourselves, and getting the human race ready for the great revelation that was to come when, "Down from the heavens, from the royal throne, leapt your all-powerful Word; into the heart of a doomed land the stern warrior leapt" (Wisdom 18:15). This was Jesus, God and man, the "bridge" that spans the gap between earth and heaven. In Jesus we have "The supreme High Priest who has gone through to the highest heaven" (Hebrews 4:14) the true Holy of Holies, of which the old one was but a shadow.

Between earth and Heaven stands death. To bridge the gap

Jesus had to destroy the power of death. He did that by going through death and rising again a new man, a glorified body, a spiritual being. Death, then, need hold no fear for us, for we also, having passed through death, will, in our turn, at the appointed time, rise again, new men and women, one with the risen person of Christ, and take our place in the kingdom of heaven.

So Jesus, the High Priest, offered himself in sacrifice, taking all our sins and sinfulness upon himself, and by his death destroyed the death-dealing power of sin. Then he went on ahead to take his place in the Trinity.

But he knew that men and women here on earth would sin and sin again. He had destroyed the power of sin and built the bridge between earth and heaven, but men and women would need to *see* that bridge, to have the act of death-destroying, the sacrifice of Jesus, actualized before their eyes. So Jesus established a new priesthood which was a continuation of his own, a share of his own, for human priests would be acting, not in their own name but in his. In this way, through the ministry of his priests, Jesus would perpetuate his sacrifice on earth. They obey his injunction: "Do this as a memorial of me" (Luke 22:19), and so repeat Jesus's own words, and speaking in his name say: "Take it and eat it, this is my body" and, "Drink all of you from this, for this is my blood, the blood of the Covenant which is to be poured out for many for the forgiveness of sins" (Matthew 26:26–8). And day in, day out, all round the world "from the rising of the sun to its setting" (Psalm 113 (112):3) Jesus's sacrifice is repeated and Jesus's bridge is built anew and men and women can always reach up to God.

In one sense we all share in Christ's priesthood if we are united to him and so share in his divine life and he lives in us. But here we are speaking of something so important, so momentous that it could not possibly have been left in any way vague, so, over and above our common share in Christ's priesthood, a group of men were set apart, especially called and consecrated to carry on Christ's ministerial priesthood to the end of time. The first to be called like this were the apostles. On the mountain Jesus picked out twelve men. (They are named in Matthew 10:1–4 and Luke 6:14–16.) The Twelve were by no means the only disciples Jesus had but they were chosen in a special way and given a distinctive office. It was to them that Jesus said: "Do this as a memorial of me" (Luke 22:19). The Apostles, in their turn, appointed others to carry on their role, and so it is to the present day.

So it is that we have priests among us, just ordinary men like everybody else, but invested with the highest and most Godlike calling and gift possible to anyone here on earth. Our priests are our bridges to God. The burden they must bear in consequence can be very, very heavy and often demands of them a tremendous degree of selfless service. The bridge is there inviting men and women to take the path to God, men and women, who, even if they do accept the invitation, often just tramp across the bridge, heedless of the burden they are placing upon it. God knows, however, and "your reward will be very great in heaven" (Matthew 5:12). God has built these bridges and there is no greater engineer than God. When the weight lies heavy upon them Jesus is there to help them to bear it, for, after all, it is *his* priesthood that they are sharing.

But *the* Bridge is Jesus Christ. He is the expression of God's love and care for us. He is the Word that was spoken at the beginning and must return to God carrying creation with him into its eternal destiny according to the plan of God.

CHAPTER ELEVEN

Out of the Mist

The evening was dull and misty and visibility very poor. What we could see was blurred and grey. The colours were quite indistinguishable. Driving slowly and carefully we arrived home safely and were glad to be in, out of the dreariness. I went up to my room and drew the curtains, shutting the dullness out.

It was quite a surprise to me, a pleasant surprise, when, the next morning I drew back my bedroom curtains and found the world bathed in sunshine. It was the same scene that I had looked at through the window the evening before, but what a difference! The shapes and forms were the same – the buildings, trees, telegraph pole and pillar box, but now they all stood out clearly and, Oh! the colours!

Yes, it was all here before but I hadn't been able to see it properly because of the mist, but when the sun came out and dispelled the mist that made the world of difference.

God was there too in the Old Testament, was there caring and loving and kind, tender even, but all too often the Deity was shrouded in mists of wrathfulness as the prophets thundered, "Woe to this one and woe to that other. For this crime and that crime I am going to hurl punishments upon you" (cf. many chapters of Isaiah, Jeremiah and Amos). This kind of language seems to strike home and make more impression than all the beautiful verses reflecting God's tenderness and caring: "Console my people, console them says your God" (Isaiah 40:1). "Ephraim, how could I part with you? Israel, how could I give you up?" (Hosea 11:8). "I have loved you with an everlasting love, so I am constant in my affection for you" (Jeremiah 31:3). There are many, many more!

Perhaps it is that: "At various times in the past and in various ways, God spoke to our ancestors through the prophets" (Hebrews 1:1), and the prophets, being human, could only muffle the words of God so that, although the message they gave was God's message, somehow the mist of human words didn't convey the fullness of God's wonderful loving relationship with us. But, "in our own time," went on the letter to the Hebrews, "the last days, he has spoken to us through his Son". Yes, "The people that walked in darkness has seen a great light. On those who live in the land of deep shadow a light has shone" (Isaiah 9:1). Jesus was that great light, "I am the light of the world, anyone who follows me will not be walking in the dark; he will have the light of life" (John 8:12).

How is it then, that we don't see Jesus like this? Many people don't know him at all. Other people have heard of him and are bored, while others feel that they ought to be more enthusiastic but just don't get past paying him mere lip service.

The sun has come up all right, and dispelled the mist, but some of us have got behind something that is casting a shadow over us so we are still in the shade and so still enveloped by the mist. It may be that, in one of many possible ways, we are just not walking in the light because we are not following Jesus. We're going some other way which is not his way. We'll never be in the light if we continue along that path.

Or there may be something wrong with our spiritual eyesight. I think this is quite common. We harbour a mental image of God of our own narrow fabrication. We think that God is a hard taskmaster, always ready to find fault, to pounce on us and to punish. If anything goes wrong we blame God and take it as a proof of God's cold indifference or worse, and this only serves to confirm our false image of God.

Jesus, we are told, is "the image of the unseen God" (Colossians 1:15) so we may be prejudiced against Jesus from the start. That is highly unfair. We make an unpleasant mask which we call "God", put it on Jesus because, after all, Jesus is

God, and then say, "Sorry, I don't really want to know you. Anyway, I can do without you."

We should go about it the other way round. Forget about all our preconceived images of God. For the moment forget about Jesus being God, if that helps. Get to know Jesus. Discover what a fantastic person he was. Read through the Gospels with an open mind and a prayerful attitude and note how caring he was, how important people were to him, people individually, not just in crowds. Notice how straight he was and how strong, how completely self-forgetting, and how bravely he "Went on ahead, going up to Jerusalem" (Luke 19:28). He was heading for Jerusalem because it was there that he was to show that "Greater love", that, "has no man than this, that he lay down his life for his friends" (John 15:13 RSV). By laying down his life for us, his friends, in the terrible way he did, he brought about our reconciliation with God, which means that we can look forward to everlasting happiness, and that makes this life make sense.

However, we won't get very far in our quest for Jesus if we try to do it all on our own. We must turn to the Holy Spirit and ask him to turn on the light for us so that we may get a glimpse of the terrific person that Jesus is. I say "is" because he is not just someone who "was", who died and has gone. No, he rose again, he is alive now, and, as he is God, we can meet God in him, not as a cold, distant overlord or judge but as Love itself. Jesus shows us God as God really is. That is what is meant by, "Jesus is the image of the unseen God". "Mirror" might have been a better translation, Jesus "reflects" the loving person that God is. The sun will have come out!

I know that all the mist won't go away as easily as that. There will be thick patches that baffle us quite a lot. The haunting bogey of "punishment" is one of these. We may point to the many instances in the Old Testament when the unfaithful people were "punished" and we may say: "There you are, you see!" We may look around in our own lives and in the lives of others and again say: "You see!" (Just think of those people today who are saying that Aids is a punishment from God, "You see!")

51

Well, what are we to think of punishment? Does God really punish us like that? Is that what our mishaps, disasters and griefs are all about? No, I don't think so. Jesus took the punishment in our stead and God doesn't punish twice. That would rubbish the Passion and Death of Jesus. After all Isaiah said: "On him lies a punishment that brings us peace" (Isaiah 53:5).

I do think, though, that quite often we punish ourselves by going away from the way that Jesus is showing us. Our own way, which is the wrong way, can lead us into dangerous places and end up in disillusionment and hurt. We can find ourselves in a very big mess.

There is also this, God's action in our lives can look like punishment when really it is caring. The way we treat those we care for can illustrate this.

I remember "punishing" a child once because she stood on her head on a piece of rock jutting out over a precipice. I made her walk beside me instead of running off and playing with her friends. I held her firmly by the hand and just would not let her go until we had passed that dangerous place. When the psalmist says, "Your right hand holds me fast" (Psalm 62:9 Grail) he was rejoicing in the security that that afforded. My youngster sulked and resisted and thought that she was being very hard done by. For my part I was trembling at the thought of what might have happened had she slipped, and what might still happen if I let her go, seeing the wayward mood that was on her.

It was one of my duties at that time to take children for long all-day outings in the mountains, and I could be powerfully strict on those occasions. Or so it might have seemed to the children who were probably glad to be free of me whenever they could. My severity was not because I wanted to be a spoil-sport, but because I didn't want any harm to come to the children. My responsibility was the greater because of their irresponsibility. We also can be wayward and irresponsible and very often we are just that, as were also the Hebrews of Old Times. So much, then, for God's wrath and thunder, it was just a proof of caring!

Jesus showed firmness too. He was outright and courageous enough to show up the Scribes and Pharisees for their hypocrisy (Matthew 22:13–33), to upset the priests by turning the traders and traffickers out of the Temple precincts: "My house will be a house of prayer. But you have turned it into a robbers' den" (Luke 19:46), and to call Herod a "fox" (Luke 13:32). Yet all these were the people who, between them, were capable of getting him crucified! He was straight too, with the Samaritan woman at Jacob's Well. He let her know that he knew full well that the man she was living with wasn't her husband (John 4:18), and he gave the people a stern warning: "If you do not repent you will all perish" (Luke 13:3). That is to say they were going the wrong way and so would not find their way into his Kingdom, or have any part in his New Covenant that would be sealed with his blood (Hebrews 9:21) because they were going along the wrong road. "Jerusalem, Jerusalem . . . how often have I longed to gather your children as a hen gathers her chicks under her wings, and you refused" (Matthew 23:37).

How often Yahweh, in the Old Testament, had promised the Covenant and warned that it could be missed. What I have been calling the "Christ-Life" or "Christ-Church" is no other than this Kingdom or Covenant, and if God seems to use wrath and thunder it is merely to express a loving desire and concern that we all find a way in.

So what I am saying in this chapter is that Jesus was the living revelation of God. This is not surprising for he is the "Word" of God. When God speaks God says, "Jesus". The principal thing that Jesus revealed was God's immense love for each one of us which is shown in God's willingness to forgive, God's desire for us to be lifted up into the eternal God-life for which we were created. In other words, what Jesus tells us is that "God loved the world so much that he gave his only Son, so that everyone who believes in him may not be lost but may have eternal life" (John 3:16).

CHAPTER TWELVE

Spirit-filled

Who is this Holy Spirit that I have mentioned several times already? God is Love, and the Holy Spirit, the Spirit of Love, is God, equal in all things to the other two divine Persons. Of the three divine persons of the Trinity, the Spirit is the hardest to form a concept of and, therefore, is the hardest to speak about. When relating to the First Person we have an image with which we are all familiar, the parent image. Traditionally we have always spoken of "God the Father". Many people prefer a mother image. Both fatherhood and motherhood come from God so both images reflect a true aspect of God. The Second Person or the Word, plunged right into humanity and became Jesus, son of Mary. There is, therefore, no need to look for an image. Jesus, himself, is the "image of the unseen God". But the Spirit is different. There is no tangible image that we can relate to. (The three images which are applied to the Spirit are a dove, the wind, and tongues of fire. We can't relate to any of these.) But everywhere we turn we meet the result of the Spirit's activity and we realize that no divine activity takes place in which the Spirit has not an important part.

It is through this, then, that we come to "sense" the living, personal "Presence" that is the Spirit, and as this presence grows more real to us, we gradually learn who the Spirit is and the need we have of this living Love who is the Third Person of the Trinity.

Even Jesus, God and all as he was, needed, as man, to be guided, moved and enabled by the Spirit and the Spirit was with him all the time. He was always Spirit-filled.

We first hear of the Spirit in connection with Jesus when God prepared a mother for the Word. That was the work of the Spirit, so from the first moment of her existence Mary, also, was Spirit-filled. Then the Spirit overshadowed Mary when she was to conceive Jesus, for, as we saw, his was no ordinary conception.

The presence of the Spirit, close to Jesus, was most obvious at his baptism. On that occasion the Spirit appeared in the form of a dove hovering over Jesus when he came up out of the water after being baptized by John (Matthew 3:16). Then we are told that Jesus was "led by the Spirit into the wilderness to be tempted by the Devil" (Matthew 4:1).

That seems a strange thing for the Spirit to do, but Jesus, the man Jesus, had to be subjected to this experience as it was to be the life-long experience of those who were to follow him in his Christ-Church. The Spirit was certainly with Jesus in the desert, and the Spirit also certainly accompanies us all through our temptations and the desert experiences of our lives.

Jesus knew well that he needed the strength and help of the Spirit and he knew that the Spirit was always with him. He began his ministry by publicly declaring: "The Spirit of the Lord has been given to me, for he has anointed me" (Luke 4:18). He was quoting from Isaiah (61:1) and applying the prophecy to himself. The Spirit never left Jesus, but directed and strengthened him throughout his human life. Jesus spoke and acted constantly by the power of the Spirit as the Gospels frequently testify. As St John said: "God gave him the Spirit without reserve" (John 3:34).

This is very important for us. If we are members of Christ's Body (Ephesians 5:30), if we are living Christ's life because he is living in us (Galatians 2:20), then we must live in the same way as he did. In that case we must be led, guided, enlightened, strengthened and enabled by the Spirit as he was, and not just obstinately do our own thing and go our own way.

Jesus promised that the Spirit would be there. He said: "I shall ask my Father and he will give you another Advocate to be with you for ever, the Spirit of Truth . . . he is with you, he is in you" (John 14:16–17). Don't be put off by the term "Advocate". That is just a translation for want of a better word. In the original Greek of St John's Gospel, the word "parakletos" is used. That was sometimes translated as "paraclete" which nobody understood. The real meaning of "parakletos" is "one who is called to the side of" (X. Leon Dufour, *Dictionary of Biblical Theology*). That is to say, someone who comes to help or support. This is absolutely the role of the Spirit.

St John kept coming back to this promise. He mentioned it four times in that breathtaking talk of Jesus at the Last Supper, which he recorded in chapters 13–17 of his Gospel. It is very beautiful and rewarding reading and well worth pondering over. In chapter 14, verse 26, John specifically says that this Advocate is the Holy Spirit: "The Advocate, the Holy Spirit whom the Father will send in my name . . ." Jesus added: "I will send him to you, but if I don't go he won't come" (cf. John 16:7).

After his resurrection, Jesus came back to this same promise and told the disciples to stay in Jerusalem until its fulfilment and, "You are clothed with power from on high" (Luke 24:49). This power the Spirit would bring them.

St Luke takes up this theme again in the Acts of the Apostles where he describes the first great sending of the Holy Spirit at the feast of Pentecost (Acts 2:1–4). "They were all filled with the Holy Spirit", he said, and told how there was a noise that "sounded like a powerful wind from heaven . . . and something appeared to them that seemed like tongues of fire; these separated and came to rest on the head of each of them."

The wind is often used as a symbol of the Holy Spirit. The word for "Spirit" in Hebrew is "ruah" which also means wind or breath. When the word "ruah" is spoken it sounds rather like a breathing noise. It is really rather an apt symbol. We can't see the wind, we can't control it, yet its power is immense when it is blowing strongly, though it can also drop to the gentlest of breezes. And breath signifies life. We read at the very beginning of the Bible, when God created humankind, that God "breathed into his nostrils a breath of life, and thus man became a living being" (Genesis 2:7).

So the Spirit was active at the creation. The Spirit was present at the Incarnation (when the Word became man). The Spirit led Jesus through all his human life and Jesus promised to send the Spirit to guide the disciples after he, Jesus, had left them. "Receive the Holy Spirit" (John 20:22), Jesus said when he appeared after he had risen from the dead, and we have that mighty coming of the Holy Spirit at Pentecost as we have just seen.

This invasion of their lives by the Holy Spirit at Pentecost worked a tremendous transformation in the early followers of Jesus. Before that they had been huddled together behind locked doors "for fear of the Jews" (John 20:19) then, all of a sudden they became brave and fearless and began going out and preaching everywhere that Jesus was Lord and had risen from the dead. It didn't even deter them when the authorities started arresting some of their number (Acts 4:3), and put Stephen, and later James, to death. (Acts 8:1 and 12:2).

No, the Christ-Church was well and rightly launched and nothing could stop it. You can read about its early days in the Acts of the Apostles. If you do, you will find in chapter 2, verses 38–39, that St Peter said: "Everyone of you must be baptized in the name of Jesus Christ for the forgiveness of your sins and you *will receive the gift of the Holy Spirit.* The promise that was made is for you and your children." We are included in that promise.

The Apostles knew that it was up to them to continue the work of Jesus, "sending the Spirit", sharing, as they did, in the .priesthood of Jesus. So they laid hands on those who believed in the Lord Jesus, in so doing they transmitted to them this gift of the Holy Spirit (Acts 8:17 and 19:6).

The laying on of hands is a very old and meaningful gesture. It was used way back in the Old Testament (Numbers 8:10 and Deuteronomy 34:9), so it was quite natural for the Apostles to make use of this gesture. Jesus himself had laid hands upon those whom he healed by the power of the Spirit (Mark 6:6). When the Apostles laid hands upon people it was visible to all that they received the Holy Spirit (Acts 8:17–18). The custom has continued in the Church to this day.

That is how it comes about that a bishop confirms people. He lays his hands upon them and prays that the Holy Spirit will come upon them. He also anoints them with especially blessed oil. This is symbolic of the work of the Holy Spirit in us, strengthening and enlightening us. Confirmation is a very important sacrament. It is the moment when young people who have been baptized in infancy, take their own responsibility, ratify the promises made in their name and really accept Jesus into their lives. The Holy Spirit is needed more than ever at this moment and is there to make them strong in their new commitment, ready to lead really Christian lives and to bear witness to Jesus before all those with whom they come in contact.

The trouble is that when we are confirmed nothing much seems to happen. Of course a lot is happening inside that we are not aware of, and strength is given that we don't feel until we need it, and then we may not realize where it came from. But perhaps much more would happen, even extraordinary things, if we had more faith and were more open to the Spirit and didn't put blocks preventing the flow of the gifts the Spirit bestows upon us. We are rather like those people who go about with headphones on, listening in to their private transistor programmes. If you talk to them they won't hear you unless they turn the set off and take off the headphones. If they don't do that they won't get your message no matter how urgent or important it may be. Neither will we get the Spirit's message if we are only wrapped up in our own thing.

We need times of quiet, silence and stillness when we can really listen to God, with everything else switched off. We need, in other words, times of prayer. Those who do listen to the Holy Spirit, who open themselves entirely to the influence of the Spirit will find their lives transformed.

The Spirit is a personal presence, but an immaterial presence. A presence who is a person who is Love, vital and active Love who meets our spirit, addresses Itself to our spirit and touches us. So it is on the level of Spirit to spirit that we human beings can relate to the Holy Spirit of God.

CHAPTER THIRTEEN

One more Station

Did you ever get out of a train at the wrong station? The next station was where you meant to get out but you got out at the one before by mistake. That is bad enough, but if you are not aware of your mistake and leave the station convinced that you have arrived at the correct place you will be pretty badly lost, especially if there is no other train to take you on further.

Many of the "Stations of the Cross" in churches are like that. They take you to the 14th station, "Jesus is laid in the tomb" – dead, finished! But the next, and most important station is just under three days further on, "Jesus rose from the dead".

If the 14th station were really the end of the road, I'm afraid our oneness with Christ would merely be a beautiful bubble. Jesus, the historical Jesus, could just be dismissed as another has-been. A good man certainly, a really extraordinary man who actually made quite a dent on the world's history, but that wouldn't help us much. A dent on history wouldn't be much good for you and me. But if he came alive again that would be quite different. It would make all the difference in the world. He couldn't be just an ordinary man. He would have to be more. Could he be divine, that is to say, could he be God?

Interestingly enough that was the whole summary of the teachings of the Apostles to the early Christians. Their whole creed was: "Jesus is risen. He is alive. Jesus is Lord." And when they said "Jesus is *Lord*", they were using a term which in their language was a title of divinity, in other words they were saying, "Jesus is alive. He is God."

Jesus passed through death and rose again resplendent. The

mighty Word of God leapt back into the Godhead, and did not return empty but "carrying out God's will succeeded in what it was sent to do" (cf. Isaiah 55:11). The divine Word returned to the Godhead united to the humanity of Jesus. This meant that for the first time a human person had been raised up into the life of the Trinity. Jesus was this first. St Paul says: "As he is the Beginning, he was first to be born from the dead" (Colossians 1:18).

He was the first but others are to follow. That was God's plan for us from the beginning. We also will pass through death and are destined to find entrance into the life of the Trinity, call it Heaven if you like. If Jesus had not been the first to rise from the dead and make that leap into the Godhead, we would never have been able to follow. "You have been taught that when we were baptized in Christ Jesus we were baptized in his death, in other words, when we were baptized we went into the tomb with him and joined him in death, so that as Christ was raised from the dead by the Father's glory, we too might *live a new life*" (Romans 6:3–4). If we accept that new life, which is a share of Christ's own life, we also will be taken up by Christ into Heaven. We must believe this. "Our faith will be 'considered' if we believe in him who raised Jesus our Lord, from the dead, Jesus who was put to death for our sins and *raised to life to justify us*" (Romans 4:25).

The question is, what exactly do we mean when we say that Jesus rose from the dead? Well, it is very difficult to say. The disciples weren't very explicit about it. They were very definite that he had risen from the dead, but instead of explaining just what that meant, they rather left us to draw our own conclusions. To begin with, if Jesus was making a leap into a totally new life, rather obviously, he didn't just get up out of the tomb, as if he had been in a deep sleep, and carry on as before. It would have been suspect if he had. People would have said that he had only fainted, lost consciousness, but not really died. No, he died all right. The Gospels make it quite clear that everybody, at the time, was quite sure of it, enemies as well as friends. But he came out of death different. Exactly what this difference was we don't really know. There are experiences which are hard to put into words, and if the disciples didn't tell us how it was that they did not immediately recognize him, at least they didn't hide the fact that they didn't. Mary Magdalene went to the Garden where he had been buried and met him there. She thought he was a gardener and asked him where he had laid the body of her Lord. It was only when he spoke to her, called her by her name, that she suddenly knew that it was he (John 20:11–18). The two disciples on their way to Emmaus were joined by a "stranger". They held a long conversation with him all about Jesus: "Starting with Moses and going through all the prophets he explained to them the passages throughout the Scriptures that were about himself." But they didn't realize that it was Jesus himself who was walking with them and talking to them. It was only when they arrived at their house and invited him in to a meal that "they recognized him at the breaking of bread" (Luke 24:11–35). This want of recognition may have been the result of a kind of spiritual blindness on the part of the disciples, because when he appeared to all the Apostles together, we are told, "He opened their minds to understand the Scriptures, and he said to them, 'So you see how it is written that the Christ would suffer *and on the third day rise from the dead*'" (Luke 24:46). They needed help to understand, and with understanding came recognition.

Then there were Jesus's curious appearances and disappearances. The power of doing this was certainly something new. He was even able to come into a room without opening the door. "In the evening of that same day, the first day of the week, the doors were closed in the room where the disciples were, for fear of the Jews. Jesus came and stood among them" (John 20:19–29). Eight days later the same thing happened again. Again we are told that the doors were closed, by which I think we can understand that they were locked because they were afraid, but Jesus didn't unlock them. Finally he rose up into the air and "a cloud took him from their sight" (Acts 1:9–11). They didn't see him any more after that. They knew, however, that he was alive. He had gone to the Father yet, according to his promise, was with them still: "Know that I am with you always; yes to the end of time" (Matthew 28:20).

This, his being alive but not visible to sight, is very important for us. Rising from the dead Jesus seems to have shed our ordinary dimensions. We can't come and go without reference to space and time. We can't pass through doors and walls. We are bound by place. That is our limitation. We can't be both here and there, in this place or that, no matter how far away, or just over there. Changing place is a whole business for us involving overcoming obstacles (such as doors and distance) and needing transport. Jesus, the risen Jesus, is not bound by place but is everywhere. God is everywhere. We call that being "omnipresent", so the man Jesus, after rising from the dead was only sharing in the divine attribute of "omnipresence", which was his right as he was also truly God.

Sharing one divine attribute he certainly shared others too. So we can say that he was not limited by time either. He was not bound by the "now" and "then", the "before" or "after", the "sooner" or "later". It is all the same to him. That is what "eternal" means. These two qualities of omnipresence and eternity explain how Jesus was, is now, and always will be. From the very beginning of creation until the end of time Jesus *is*. The fact of his not being timebound means that the past is no more of a problem to him than the present or the future. So although he was born in time as a man, as God he is eternally present. As his divinity and his humanity are totally blended, even his manhood is no longer bound by time. This is why we can speak of the pre-existence of Jesus in the world, even from the beginning of creation. That makes him hold the central position of all things created, and his presence to fill the universe in its entirety, spacewise and timewise. But he had to break through death to come to this. That is why the next station is so important. If they had just laid him in the tomb and he had stayed there that would have been the end indeed. The Christ-

Church would not have made sense and we would have had no pledge of our own resurrection and no hope of going to heaven.

As it is Jesus is in direct contact with us. We should pray for the gift of awareness of this so as not to miss him. He also comes to us under many different disguises. We don't always recognize him. Perhaps we too suffer from a kind of spiritual blindness which makes it difficult for us to discern his presence. We think we are speaking to a "gardener"; (cf. John 20:15) or some "fellow traveller" (cf. Luke 24:15), and perhaps we shunt him off, forgetting that he said: "What ever you do to the least of my little ones you do unto me" (Matthew 25:40). We are often so thick-skinned, insensitive and short-sighted that we are totally unaware of Jesus in our midst, even closer to us than we are to ourselves.

If it is hard to recognize him in casual encounters perhaps we will do better when we are praying with others; that is, meeting together specifically in view of finding him. After all he did say, "Where two or three meet in my name I shall be there with them" (Matthew 18:20). This is true of simple reunions when we are God-conscious and God-seeking, it is even more true when we meet for the "breaking of bread". Many of Jesus's contemporaries refused to follow him any more when he told them that he was going to give them his flesh to eat and his blood to drink. They were shocked at the idea. "This is intolerable language", they said. "How could anyone accept it?" (John 6:60). They were looking only at the crude interpretation of his words. He meant something equally real but on quite a different level.

It is his risen, or glorified body and blood that he shares with us, and that is of such a nature that, while it is really and truly his body and blood that we receive in holy communion, it is a body and blood of which we have no other experience, we have nothing to compare it with. It is his living self that comes to us to unite us to himself and this is quite other than that crude meaning taken by those earth-bound people who couldn't make a leap into a higher sphere of understanding. This is the leap of faith but if we make it it means that Jesus comes right into our lives and beings and makes us one with him.

So let us not think that Jesus just lived and died 2,000 years ago and that was it. Let us not forget that he rose again and is alive today. He reached that last and important station! We can't see or hear him now with our this-world eyes and ears, but if we seek him faithfully in his kingdom in this world we will see and hear him fully when he takes us through death with him into the everlasting Kingdom of Heaven. It is up to each one of us to make sure we don't miss the train or get out at the wrong station.

Part III: *God's Adopted Children*

We think of ourselves as men and women engaged in the various business of human living. Everything that goes on within the horizons of life in this world concerns us nearly. There is, however, a wider horizon, on a very different plane, which concerns us even more nearly; namely, our supernatural condition of adopted sons and daughters of God. This state did not come to us naturally or automatically but thanks to the life and death of the Word of God made man: "God sent his son . . . to enable us to be adopted as sons" (Galatians 4:5–6).

Jesus's life and death "enable" us to be adopted sons and daughters of God, but do not force us against our wills. There is every advantage for us in accepting the invitation and becoming adopted children of God, but we must also accept the terms and conditions and the means offered to us. For this we may have choices and options to make and have to be careful to get our priorities right. Then, in all peace and confidence, we will be able to await the coming of Christ to take us home to himself. "It was his purpose to bring a great many of his sons and daughters into glory" (Hebrews 2:10).

How we are involved in all this, and different aspects of this involvement will be considered in the remaining chapters of this book.

CHAPTER FOURTEEN

Echoes

"Coo-ee," I shouted between cupped hands and my voice rolled down into the valley. "Oo-eee -eee -eee" came back the echo from the surrounding mountains. I laughed and called again. Again the echo of my voice came back to me.

In my own puny way I was imitating God. "Let there be . . .," boomed God and the mighty Word of God went forth into the deep, deep nothingness, and light and stars and birds and beasts and humankind echoed back from every particle of crystallized Word that twirled and twinkled now in the immensity of space. For everything that *is* echoes God and shines back an image of the Godhead to its maker, especially men and women, for, "God created man in the image of himself" (Genesis 1:27).

Made in the image of God how can we do other than reflect something of God? This image should be perfect: God's love, God's beauty, God's creativity, in fact all God's attributes. But this image is fragmented. We don't all reflect the same piece, and often what we do reflect is sadly distorted, blurred and nearly, if not totally, unrecognizable.

According to God's plan, in the "fullness of time" (Ephesians 1:10 RSV) all things will be brought together. Then, like pieces of a jigsaw, or rather, a beautiful mosaic, the face of Christ, the Word of God made man, will be seen in all its beauty.

God called us all into existence, each one a faint echo of a whisper of Godself. An echo returns to the one who initiates the sound and we return to God. And all these echoed whispers will surely make a mighty chorus that will be marvellous to hear because it will be a love song – our love song and God's, for God is Love and all God's calls are whisperings of love.

We have no conception of what God has prepared for us in the Kingdom of Heaven. That will be the big surprise, but to be capable of living in the divine atmosphere we must harmonize with Christ, the eternal Word of God so that there will be only one song, Christ's song, and we will be able to sing it with him because we will be one with him, sharing his life. He living in us. That is the invitation. That is the meaning of life. That is what we were created for. That is why we were created in "the image and likeness of God"; destined to be one with the Son who is the visible "image of the unseen God" (Colossians 1:15).

God is not only invisible but transcendent, that is to say totally "other". God is way out and beyond us in a way that we could never comprehend. There had to be a link, a bridge and, as we have already seen (Chapter Ten) that link was Jesus. "No one has gone up to heaven except the one who has come down from heaven, the Son of Man who is in heaven" (John 3:13). This Son of Man is Jesus, God and Man, come down from heaven yet still is in heaven. In reflecting Jesus whom we see as man, we are also reflecting God who is invisible.

Jesus is a model we can see and imitate as he is like us. He felt as we do. He was tired (John 4:6, Luke 8:23). He was angry (Mark 3:5, John 2:15–17). He was afraid (Mark 14:33). He loved (Mark 10:21, John 19:26, 17:23, 13:1) and wept because he lost someone he loved (John 11:36). He was disappointed (Matthew 23:37). He was surprised (Luke 7:9). He was exasperated (Mark 9:19). Above all he was compassionate (Mark 8:2ff, Luke 7:13, Mark 6:34, Matthew 14:14). These are only some examples of Jesus's human reactions, as you roam through the Gospels surely you will find many other instances.

Jesus used all his human emotions, under the guidance of the Spirit, to further God's glory and the coming of God's Kingdom. We go wrong and deviate from the Christ-Life in us when we do not allow ourselves to be Spirit-led but use our faculties and emotions to further our own selfish ends. We do this in our short-sightedness, thinking we can see clearly, and our want of faith, failing to trust in the goodness of God's plans.

Because of this short-sightedness and want of faith we often have to struggle against our own inclinations and wills. We may have to abandon our own plans for ourselves and the road we would like to follow. We have to accept God's lordship over us and that means accepting people, events, situations and circumstances as they come. I do not mean that we should have a fatalistic, passive attitude and shouldn't strive for a better world, but I do mean that when there are people, events, situations and circumstances in our own lives over which we have no control, then we must bow in acceptance. This acceptance, even in little things, can be excruciatingly difficult. Fortunately, Jesus gave us an example here too. Jesus was not short-sighted or untrusting but, as man, he had to overcome normal human repugnance and resistance to accepting his frustrations and especially his crucifixion and death. This repugnance was so great that in his agony in the Garden, "he prayed ever more earnestly, and his sweat fell to the ground like great drops of blood" (Luke 22:44).

You often hear of people coming out in a cold sweat when they are apprehensive and afraid but I have never heard of anyone else being so hard-pressed that they actually sweated blood. "He prayed the more earnestly", and what was his prayer? "Father . . . take this cup from me." But he added: "Nevertheless, let your will be done, not mine" (Luke 22:42). In passing I might say here that it was not Jesus's suffering that was what God willed but our salvation. The sufferings of Jesus were the means by which that was brought about. Jesus accepted the means so that God's will for the happiness of humankind might be assured.

To me the Agony, with the sweat of blood, in the Garden of Gethsemane, is echoed in the many, often very difficult, acceptances we have to make, and which cause those teeth-grinding, sleepless nights of struggle with ourselves, against our self-will, our revolts and our rages. It may be a shock, disappointment or failure. We may feel we are being exploited or treated with downright injustice. The situation may be aggravated by our own greed or jealousy, ambition or lust. We may be unforgiving or seeking revenge. We may have to accept the result of an accident or the onslaught of a serious illness either in ourselves or someone dear to us. It may be the loss of a loved one or our own declining health or approaching death. Or it may just be the ups and downs and little frustrations of daily life.

Whatever it is (and each one has his or her own personal version of difficult acceptance), we cannot change the situation. There is only one thing to do and that is to allow the Spirit to lead us through the tempest and turmoil until finally we come out into the smooth waters of God's loving plan for us, even though the getting there may make us (nearly but not quite) sweat blood. The end of our torment will finally come but not before the end of our resistance.

God called us into existence. God is calling us to eternal happiness in union with Jesus, the Eternal Word. God calls us in many, and often very unexpected, ways and through many very difficult situations. It is up to us to listen, hear God's voice and echo back: "Here I am, Lord. Is it I, Lord? I hear you calling in the night." (cf. Isaiah 6. *Lord of Light*, N. American Literature Resources, Dan Schutte, S.J. [St Louis], Epoc Publishers.)

Why, then, is it that we are so short-sighted? Why can't we see clearly? What makes it so difficult for us to see God clearly enough to be able to trust? There is a smog that I have already referred to, a smog that is really sin. It blinds us and distorts our understanding and falsifies our wills. This smog plays a very big part in our lives. Perhaps it would be well to look a little more closely at it in the next chapter.

CHAPTER FIFTEEN

Smog

I picked up the paper one day and a headline caught my eye: "20,000 fish die in a polluted river". I forget what it was that caused the pollution. I thought how sad that kind of thing was, and wondered how many other creatures had been affected by poisonous matter seeping into that river and other waterways. How many sea-birds have been killed by oil slicks? And how many acres of fine forests have been destroyed by acid rain? The list of damage to nature is very long. How lovely it would be if the sea were always clean, the sands safe and the countryside uncontaminated.

My thoughts turned in other directions and I sighed when I thought of all the bag-snatching, shop-lifting, house-breaking, not to mention baby-bashing and more, that goes on all the time. Why all this? There always has been crime of all sorts, but why? Why should there be all this crime? Reflecting upon all this I could find no other reason than that the very rock-bottom cause of all human wrongdoing is original sin. The question is, what exactly do we mean by "original sin"?

Turning it over I think of it as a kind of pollution, a contamination, a smog that lies between humanity and the Christ-Life. To make a comparison: on the physical level, factory chimneys, exhaust pipes, nuclear waste units and what have you, belch fumes and pollution into the atmosphere from the cities of the earth. This is considered to be a criminal offence as it is a poisonous danger that must be reduced and, if possible, totally eliminated. I say "if possible" because there is an "if". If we are to make progress we will certainly also make mistakes. That seems inevitable. Sometimes these mistakes are culpable because they are due to carelessness, negligence, cutting corners for greed, selfishness, laziness, etc. And so, although we are ecology conscious and aim at having a pure atmosphere to breathe, we continue to pollute, not only the air, but the rivers, the sea, the fields and the whole environment and, whether we like it or not, we live in this environment and breathe this air, and toxic elements invade our lungs and our blood-streams, and affect everything from our joints to our brain cells.

It is not only the factories and power stations of our industrial areas or the pesticides of the countryside that discharge filth into the environment. Any un-Christlike actions, thoughts or intentions of men and women, their passions and hates, ambitions, jealousies, selfishness and greed, release into the spiritual atmosphere, fumes, every bit as toxic as those science can monitor. From the time the first men and women (call them Adam and Eve if you like) walked on earth, the human race has been evolving, developing and progressing, but not without the co-operation of our own free-thought processes and choices. We have been making progress, and mistakes, from the very beginning. Often these mistakes have been downright culpable wrong choices, and they have cut across or by-passed God's plan for us disastrously. In particular this was the case at the very beginning of human existence. The Bible account of the eating of the forbidden fruit is symbolic of some very wrong choice made by our first ancestors. Something in human nature was warped by this wrong choice. This has affected us ever since. Our spiritual atmosphere, like the physical one has been polluted. Whether we like it or not, we are born into this polluted atmosphere, this spiritual smog, and it penetrates our whole being and makes us sinners, so we also commit sin.

This does *not* mean that we just can't help it. The tendency is there, certainly, but we are not automatic robots. We must take the responsibility for our own acts, because we are free, and, I'm afraid, our acts are often culpable. This spiritual smog, as I understand it, is "original sin". It is an obstacle between ourselves and God and interferes with our total union with

Christ. That Christ dealt with sin by sacrificing his life and, in so doing, reconciled us to God, we have already seen. Thanks to Jesus, the flood waters of Baptism are able to wash away the dirt left in us by this smog and so we are given a good start at the same time that we are adopted into the family of God.

Unfortunately we don't stay all that spiritually clean. We may have been cleansed but we still live in the atmosphere polluted by smog and, only too easily, we add more smog of our own making. Some of this we like to put down to human error, but much of it is just culpable, our own fault.

There is such a thing as genuine human error, but so much of our so-called "human error" could be avoided if we wanted. If we took a little more care, if we didn't allow ourselves to be influenced by very questionable motives such as over-ambition, greed, jealousy, selfishness, passion, etc. much "human error" could be avoided. "Human error" is a great excuse but the real name for our wrongdoing is "sin". What makes it wrong is that it runs contrary to God's plan for us. It, so to speak, puts spokes in God's wheels, and therefore it is harmful to ourselves or to others. That's what we mean when we say that a thing is "sinful".

God has told us what is right and wrong in the Ten Commandments. You can read in Exodus, chapter 20, about how God gave the commandments to Moses. They are rather like the "maker's instructions" telling how best the thing works! They may seem negative in tone but actually they are dictated by love and protectiveness. For example, if God says, "Thou shalt not kill", or "Thou shalt not steal" etc. God is not only saying that you and I must not do these things, but that *other people may not do them to you or to me*, and that because of the great love God has for us. Seen from that angle we can see the point of the commandments, can't we?

But what if we do sin? Is everything mucked up for us? Can we never reach the wonderful destiny prepared for us. Can God forgive us? God is Love and Love can't help forgiving. So if we sin we turn to God and apologize. We admit that we have done wrong, that it was our own fault and we humbly ask pardon, and we can be absolutely sure that we will be restored to God's friendship just as if nothing had ever happened. In Chapter Twenty we will be talking about this again. So in spite of all the smog that surrounds us, it is still possible for humankind to become Christkind, so we should never lose heart.

CHAPTER SIXTEEN

A Drop of Water

Mummy was beaming, Daddy looked proud. Godmother was very important, Godfather was shy. The grandparents were doting, while aunts and uncles fussed and fidgeted. Little brother and sister peeped and peered when they weren't racing up and down the aisle and, with a bit of luck and a well-timed last feed, baby wasn't bawling. Baby, of course, was what it was all about. Presently the priest arrived and the ceremony began. Prayers were said, a candle was lighted, rituals performed, but the high point of the ceremony was when, pouring water over baby's head, at the same time the priest addressed the child by his or her *name*, and said: "I baptize you in the name of the Father, and of the Son, and of the Holy Spirit." And God said: "I have called you by your *name*, you are mine" (Isaiah 43:1). "You are my son, my daughter, today I have become your father" (Psalm 2:7). And God really had! For baby now, was not only the child of his or her parents, but had been received into the Family of God by divine adoption. Not just an adoption like human adoption when the family name, rights and inheritance are bestowed upon a child, although, he or she cannot share blood relationship or physical resemblance. Divine adoption actually infuses a share of the divine life into the person who is baptized and the "image and likeness of God" shines forth.

Baby had now been introduced into the Christ-Life and it is interesting to note that the pouring of water over the child's head, at the same time as the words of baptism were pronounced, was the sign or symbol used to express the inflow of divine life into baby.

Plunged into the waters of Baptism humankind is united to the death of Christ, and then, sharing his Resurrection, is raised to a higher life and is taken into the life of the Trinity as adopted sons and daughters. The eternal light of God, symbolized by the sun, shines upon the newly baptized. This was made possible by the death of the Son upon a tree. And, once more, the Spirit of Love is there, hovering over our divine adoption for "God so loved the world" that the Son died upon the tree so that the light of God might shine upon us eternally

The first mention of water in the Bible is at the very beginning of Genesis when, at the creation, "God's Spirit hovered over the water" (Genesis 1:2). Life, as we saw in Chapter 4, is believed to have originated in water so it is little wonder that water should be a symbol of life. In fact the absence of water means death. I need not spell that out; we are all to aware of the horrors of famine in the world to be in any doubt about it. What we are not so conscious of is the sadness of the privation of spiritual life. That is perhaps why God also chose water to be the sign of that higher life.

The water theme all through the Old Testament was foretelling this gift of Christ-Life, and when the time came for it to be officially given to us, it was under the sacramental sign of water that it was given.

Water not only symbolizes life, it also cleanses. We have the Biblical story of Noah when the Flood washed away sin and sinners (Genesis 6:17). Speaking of this, St Peter said: "That water is a type of the baptism which saves you now" (I Peter 3:21). In the Bible, sin and wickedness of all kinds are referred to as something dirty: "A land unclean because of the foulness of the natives . . . and the abominations with which their impurities have filled it" (Ezra 9:11). Rather strong language! We know that dirt is closely linked with disease and death, hence the power in the symbol of water for washing: cleansing is life-giving. "A fountain shall be opened for the House of David and the citizens of Jerusalem, for sin and impurity" (Zechariah 13:1). So the emphasis on the water symbol is positive, the flood itself may have been destructive but it was cleansing, hence life-giving. This is all very important to us as, somehow or other (as we saw in Chapter 15, we are all born tainted with sin. "You know I was born guilty, a sinner from the moment of conception" (Psalm 51 (50):5).

The Hebrews fleeing from the slavery of Egypt were saved from their enemies by passing through the waters of the Red Sea. Until then they were being pursued and were in danger, but after the waters had closed behind them a dark chapter of their history was also closed, finally closed, and they could set out for the Promised Land recognizing God as their saviour and Lord. "The sons of Israel had marched through the sea on dry ground, walls of water to right and to left of them . . . That day Yahweh rescued Israel from the Egyptians . . . and the people venerated Yahweh" (Exodus 14:29–31). This experience of *passing through the water* which marked the beginning of the Hebrews becoming the Chosen People is very significant. It foreshadows our experience of *passing through the waters of baptism* and so becoming the Children of God.

This theme of life-giving water recurs time and time again in Scripture as if God wanted to stress both our need for it and the assurance that it would be given. "I will pour water out on the thirsty soil, streams on the dry ground . . . They shall grow like grass where there is plenty of water, like poplars by running streams" (Isaiah 44:3). "And you will draw water joyfully from the springs of salvation" (Isaiah 12:3).

And soon we find the living water identified with Yahweh, which is why turning away from God leaves us without "water" all that is essential for life. "Those who turn from you (Yahweh) will be uprooted from the land since they have abandoned the fountain of living water" (Jeremiah 17:13).

This idea of living water being associated with Jesus – who was the Word of God – was taken up by him when speaking to the woman by Jacob's Well. Jesus said: "If you only knew what God is offering and who it is who is saying to you, 'Give me a drink', you would have been the one to ask and he would have given you living water . . . anyone who drinks the water that I shall give will never thirst again. The water that I shall give shall turn into a spring inside him, welling up to eternal life" (John 4:10–14).

This "living water" that Jesus is offering is none other than a share in is own divine life which henceforth will flow in us and through us to eternal life. Through the waters of baptism we become the sons and daughters of God. That is what "a drop of water" does for us!

At this point two questions might come to mind. First: If the divine life is not given to us without our choosing to accept it, why baptize a baby who is unable to make a choice? Second: If the gift of divine adoption, a share in the divine life, is necessary if we are to become Christkind, in the Family of God, and baptism is the way it is conferred, what about all those people who were never baptized, who have never heard of baptism or will never get a chance of being baptized?

Well, to start with the baby. A baby doesn't know that it needs to be fed, clothed, bathed etc. nor does it have any choice in the matter. If neglected it will just die. An infant will cry when it is hungry but it does not know consciously why it is crying. Neither does it know that when it is sick a doctor should be consulted and medicine or treatment given. Yet what parents would wait to consult the child before giving it all these things? They will even submit the child to surgery if necessary, in which case it is they, and not the infant, who will sign the permission for the operation to be performed. The parents take total responsibility for their child until such time as he or she is able to assume his or her own responsibility. In the same way they take responsibility for the spiritual needs of their child and therefore they request that the flood-waters of baptism should cleanse their child of smog, and more important, that he or she should be received into the Family of God. When the child does reach the age for personal responsibility then he or she must ratify the decisions taken, the faith professed and the promises made in his or her name. Or he or she is free to just cancel everything. Any who do this are personally responsible for the loss they sustain. No one else has taken anything from them. But in the same way that parents train their children to get the best chances possible in life, sending them to school and many other things they themselves wouldn't have chosen and may protest about, so also the parents should teach their children about the immense gift they have received, and train them in all that pertains to the Christ-Life, and so give them the best chance possible of making the right choices and avoiding getting choked by smog.

Now the question of the unbaptized: let us suppose that you want to travel from A to B which is quite a distance. You have a good car and the motorway goes all the way. What's more, you are a member of the AA or RAC and there is no shortage of petrol. Your journey should be successful. Now, some folk don't have good cars, perhaps just a moped or pedal bike. The motorway is not open for them so they can't travel on it, but there are plenty of other roads, and side roads, and although it may take longer or be rather more difficult, they *can* arrive. Again, there are those people who don't have as much as a bike or even the fare for public transport. So they walk. That's really hard work but it's not impossible. We all know the story of the hare and the tortoise and the race they ran. The hare had by far the best chances to win but he didn't use them and the tortoise came in first. You, with the car, may be a reckless driver who does not obey the Highway Code or take notice of traffic signals, so you may very well end up in hospital, in prison or dead.

You might still think that it's not fair that some people have cars, others bikes and others nothing at all. Actually we can't judge what anyone has or has not, first of all because appearances are often deceptive and secondly because God is not limited or restricted in any way as to the distribution of gifts. There are certainly extra-sacramental as well as sacramental ways of receiving divine gifts, ways that we know nothing about. All I can say is that baptism is the official way of obtaining Christ-Life and we should be very grateful for having that revealed: "I tell you most solemnly, unless a man is born through water and the Spirit, he cannot enter the kingdom of God" (John 3:5). "Go . . . make disciples of all the nations; baptize them in the name of the Father and of the Son and of the Holy Spirit" (Matthew 28:19). "He who believes and is baptized will be saved" (Mark 16:16).

We should also remember that those to whom much has been given will have much to answer for, much will be required of them. "The Spirit blows where ever he pleases" (John 3:8), and

"Many who are first will be last, and the last, first" (Matthew 19:30).

One thing is sure and certain, even baptism isn't an automatic guarantee of eternal life. Not only must the baptized person ratify his or her baptism and personally accept the responsibilities involved, but he or she must live like Christ: "You must live your whole life according to the Christ you have received" (Colossians 2:6). "We can be sure that we are in God only when the one who claims to be living in him is living the same kind of life as Christ lived" (1 John 2:5–6). Or again: "Be renewed in the spirit of your minds, and put on the new nature, created after the likeness of God in true righteousness and holiness" (Ephesians 4:24 RSV). "In your minds you must be the same as Christ Jesus" (Philippians 2:5). That Christmind can best be summed up in one word, "Compassion". Only the compassionate can belong to Christkind.

CHAPTER SEVENTEEN

Christopher

There is an old legend that tells of a young pagan who, wishing to become a Christian, asked a spiritual master what he should do. The master told him to build a hut beside a river at a point where travellers often crossed its waters. For the love of Christ the young man was to carry travellers across the river. As he was very tall and powerfully built this was no difficult task and with great zeal he set himself to perform this act of charity.

As time went on it all got a bit boring and he couldn't really see much point in it. Then, one stormy night, when he was just settling down to sleep, there came a gentle knock at his door. It was a child, a little boy, asking to be carried across the river. Grumbling a bit and saying that a child like that shouldn't be out at that time of night, the young man swung the little lad on to his shoulders and set out to wade across the fast-running current. As he advanced the child seemed to grow heavier and heavier until, on reaching the middle of the stream, he felt he could go no further. "Christ, help me!" he called in fervent prayer. Immediately new strength came to him and without any effort he found himself on the other side of the river. The child then blessed him and disappeared. It was only then that the young man realized that he had been carrying Christ disguised as a little boy. When he recounted his adventure, his spiritual master said: "You have carried Christ. From now on you shall be called 'Christopher'." The name means "Christbearer".

Some people think the story is true and that our young man was the St Christopher who is now the patron saint of travellers. Others think that it is just a tale and St Christopher a myth. It doesn't matter really. There is so much truth to be gathered from the story that fact or parable is of no great importance.

One thing we can get out of this story is the truth that whatever we do for others we are really doing for Christ who lives in them. Jesus told us this when he said: "Whatever you do unto the least of my little ones you do it unto me" (Matthew 25:40). That is a beautiful thought and one that we could mull over for a long time and act upon with great profit. However, there is another way of looking at it which is also very deep and very enriching. That is that we can all be Christophers, or Christbearers, and it is Christ living in us that we take to others.

To grasp something of what this means let's take a look at some other "Christophers" that might come to mind. Thinking like this I came up with the altar vessels – the chalice and paten (or communion plate) that are used for the Eucharist. They bear the bread and wine that are transformed into the Body and Blood of Christ that are given to us in Communion. Yes, but these are inanimate things, they hold Christ but there is no union with him. They remain apart from him, it is just a case of juxtaposition.

Then there is Mary. Ah, she was the "Christopher" *par excellence* when she carried him in her womb, in her arms and upon her knee. Here there was truly union, he was flesh of her flesh and blood of her blood in that closest of unions, mother and child. Mary's union with Christ went far deeper than just a mother and child relationship. He came that we "may have life and have it abundantly" (John 10:10 RSV), and the life we were to have was that supernatural life that is a share in his own divine life. St Paul says: "I live now not with my own life but with the life of Christ who lives in me" (Galatians 2:20). If St Paul could say that, how much more could Mary. When the unborn Christ was living in her physically, certainly he lived in her spiritually as well, filling her with a share of his divine life. With this life he continued to live in her even after his birth, when, physically, he was living a separate life. This divine life he offers to us as well so that we also may use Paul's words, and truly live with the life of Christ who lives in us.

84

In my book *Grassroots to God* (Collins, 1980) I spoke of "outer" and "inner" prayer. Here I would speak of "outer" and "inner" spirituality. "Outer" spirituality is when we have a relationship with God, or Jesus or the Holy Spirit, as being outside of ourselves. They may be very near to us, very close indeed, but it is a relationship between two separate people. I may look upon God as a father, or a mother, or upon Jesus as a brother, a friend, a saviour, the Good Shepherd, a lover or whatever way my devotion dictates, and it is with this other that I try to develop a relationship. That is all very good and prayerful. But "inner" spirituality goes deeper than that.

In "inner" spirituality I do not seek God or Jesus outside of myself but I seek a union right within me. It is in my "Heart" (which has nothing to do with my physical heart), that centre and core of my very being, that inmost cell of myself where everything that is "me" is concentrated, it is there that I meet God and, through the almost incredible gift of God, share that divine life that makes me one with Christ, a child of God and heir to eternal life.

This life was won for me on Calvary. It is a share of that same life that melted into humanity (as heat melts wax and wax becomes fire), in the humanity of Jesus in Mary's womb. When Mary pronounced her "Fiat" – that is, her acceptance of her motherhood of God – God and man became one in the person of Jesus. The seed was sown in virgin soil by the Holy Spirit and in due time a sapling Christ looked out upon the world.

One humanity was not enough. He wished to be in all humanity, everywhere and at all times, and Mary's work it is to conceive and bring him forth in every one of us who will yield his or her humanity to him. That is the meaning of Mary's motherhood of us. When Christ is born in us we become one with him, and as he is her child, we also are her children.

That may sound like very fine words, beautiful theory, but, in practice what does it all mean? How do I *know* that I am identified with Christ, that I am one with him, having a share of his divine life coursing, so to speak, through my veins? If this is true it is absolutely stupendous. "Christ lives in me," St Paul said. So, if that is so, he also moves in me, works, prays and suffers in me. He thinks with my mind, sees with my eyes, touches with my hands, speaks with my lips. With my ears he listens to others, with my feet he treads this earth bearing the Good News of the Kingdom to those I meet. "How lovely on the mountains are the feet of those who bring good news" (Isaiah 52:7). With my heart Christ loves. He loves the Godhead and he loves all my fellow men and women. In me he adores, he intercedes, he reconciles man to God. But this is incredible! It must be the hysterical excesses of some fanatic. No, this is what Christianity is all about, this is the meaning of the Christ-Life that makes us Christkind, this is what happened to you and me when we were baptized and became the children of God, God's son or daughter, one with God's only son. Have we then just left our Christianity in the attic? Can we not open up and believe the wonderful things God has done for us?

Really *believing* can be difficult. It's quite easy to "believe" in God somewhere out there and that we forget about most of the time. It's comparatively easy to believe in Jesus, the man of Nazareth 2,000 years ago, a safe distance away. It's even fairly easy to believe in the Risen Christ truly present in the Eucharist in church once a week or so, the other side of the town. It's when he comes right up close to me, nearer than that, within me, in my Heart of hearts, his life entwined with mine that I cry, "Hold! this is impossible, I can't believe it." "Why do you doubt, oh you of little faith?" (Matthew 8:26).

No wonder my Christianity is so flat, my spiritual life so drab, religion such a bore when I won't believe that my life, no matter how dull, how limited and insignificant, can be an extension of the divine life of Jesus Christ Our Lord. Of course there is difficulty about believing if we want everything black and white and scientifically proved. Not only that but it must accommodate our love of pleasure, and tendency to take the line of least resistance. It is by *faith* that we must all live and by faith we are justified.

Believing couldn't always have been easy for Mary. I wonder if she ever looked at Jesus and thought, "Can it be true? Is it possible that this, my little boy, is truly my God?" Perhaps she did. She certainly thought things out as we are told she "pondered all these things in her heart" (Luke 2:20, 2:51). There was no doubting at Cana (John 2:1–10). No, she never faltered even though her faith took her to the foot of the Cross and gave her the strength to "stand" there (John 19:25).

We just have to hold on in faith to the conviction that all the good news of the coming of Christ into the world and into our lives is true. Let's read and re-read about it in the New Testament. We may not see or hear anything. We may not feel anything, but faith is just that. "Blessed are you who have not seen but have believed" (John 20:29). One day all will be clear.

In the meantime we must try to grow in awareness of this presence of Christ in us. We do that by paying attention to it, reflecting on it and talking to God about it. And then live our lives as Christ would live them in us.

CHAPTER EIGHTEEN

Hand-in-Hand

There's no need to speak when you're holding hands. Of course you can if you like but there's no need to, or you may be listening. But just holding hands says it all.

Children naturally hold their parents' hands. They just trot along beside them, safe and happy. Maybe they sometimes run off a little way and something, a big dog or a group of rough-looking toughs perhaps, might frighten them. A speedy return to the comforting grip of the big, warm hand round the little one and all is well.

Young lovers hold hands and how much is exchanged just by the touch of those two hands, the one in the other. Friends grasp hands when meeting, especially after a period of absence. And Darby and Joan who each knows all the other has to say, just sit hand-in-hand and know it all, all over again and are at peace.

In this book I keep on talking about the Christ-Life and being Christkind, accepting the share of divine life that Christ is offering us, and belonging to the Family of God but so far, I've said nothing at all about our relationship with this Christ whose life we share. You might almost get the impression that the "belonging" I'm talking about is something like the "belonging" to a club, or the crew of a ship or a group of passengers, or someting like that, situations where you would have no intimate relationship with the boss, the chairperson or captain. That is not at all the case with the Christ-Church. This is not a club, a ship, a business concern or whatever. It is a life, a life shared with a person, the divine person of Christ. How can a life be shared without there being an intimate relationship between those sharing it?

The child, to a certain extent, shares its parents' life, having received it from them. Young lovers long passionately to share their lives with each other. Darby and Joan have shared theirs many a year, and friendship also is a form of sharing. In all these cases so much of that sharing is expressed and exchanged by holding hands.

We, too, can hold hands with Christ, and have so much to gain by doing so, and we can do it all the time. We usually call this "prayer". In *Grassroots to God*, I treated with the subject of prayer and its different forms at some length. I will not repeat in this book all that I said in that other one. But neither can I leave the subject of relationship with Christ and let it look like a kind of formality, lives in juxtaposition, or something very impersonal, so I will reserve just this one chapter to speaking about it.

The importance of our close relationship with Christ is the first thing I want to stress. The informality of it is the second. If we don't keep this sharing and exchanging between ourselves and Christ flowing, if we let go his hand and wander off, we risk drifting further and further away from him, like lost children, estranged lovers or a bereaved Darby or Joan. We might forget the beauty, richness and happiness of the Christ-Church and the importance of being members of it. We might lower our sights and opt for fulfilment in the natural order only. We might begin to doubt that there is so very much more to come. Our spiritual vision may fade and we may be deluded into believing that we have nothing to look forward to other than fizzling out in a big black hole. How horrible!

Prayer is essential to keeping alive and brightly burning that vision of other things, Christ-things, that vision that we call faith, and the deep-seated peace that goes with it.

Spiritual writers of the past have given us great help in their works on prayer but they have also done us a disservice when they write of prayer as "spiritual exercises". That might have matched the mentality of another age, but, I think today it is off-putting, as if prayer was necessarily something arduous, if not painful, and decidedly difficult. I'm not denying the difficulties

89

we can be up against in prayer, formal prayer that is, the kind of prayer we have to work at and give regular time to. I wrote about this kind of prayer in *Grassroots to God*. It is very necessary if we are going to build up the kind of on-going relationship that I'm talking about here. And that, in turn, when we have got into the way of it, will make our formal prayer much easier.

Here, however, I want to talk about on-going prayer, or the kind of constant background prayer that goes on more or less silently nearly all the time. Some people nowadays need constant background music. Without it they feel lonely, they can't work or study, they get bored or even just a little scared. I think this background prayer I'm trying to talk about is a little like that music. Only, I think prayer works better than music. (Though, of course, perhaps that music, if of the right kind and used properly may help the background prayer. That rather depends on each person.) Such prayer is a continual attitude towards Christ which may be described as a "hand-in-hand" relationship.

You do not always consciously revert to it, you may have to be attending to other business, but it's never far away. When you do want to revert to it, or just want to be sure that Christ is there you only have to, so to speak, squeeze his hand a little, just a thought and it's OK. At first you may find this rather artificial and unreal but little by little it grows on you and you are more or less, at least half conscious of it all the time. It's rather like working or reading in a room you share with someone else. You can't be talking all the time, you've other things to do, but you are aware of the other person's presence, at least at the back of your mind, and if you are fond of that person you would miss him or her terribly if he or she went away.

And does Christ respond? Of course he does if you are attentive enough to notice it. It may come as a breeze, or a flower that gives you joy, the smile of a friend and you can see Christ smile behind it. It may be in the tear of a child, or the sigh of an old person, or a little grey cloud in the sky or elsewhere.

You may be in doubt about something, you hastily consult Christ and somehow or other the answer is there. You may be annoyed and yet, you know you're being foolish, he's telling you so. Or maybe you're happy, just happy for no reason at all, no reason you know of, but, you know he is there, so you nod him a thanks or blow him a kiss and get on with your job and you find that, that day, it's not as hard as you thought – he's with you, hand-in-hand.

It's just the realization of the presence of Christ around me and in me and on all sides of me, in those I meet and in events that affect me. A presence of God that affects my values, influences my choices and options, controls my moods, prompts me to be available or hold back that unkind word or thought, a *knowing* that he is there.

And if he is there I need not say anything. In silence I can listen to his silence, a silence that can tell me so much, teach me so much, strengthen me, calm me, control me. Nothing is said but somehow I *know* and although I may be busy, or worried, sad or upset, deep, deep down inside, underneath all that I *know*, and I am at peace.

And then, holding his hand, I can think about what I know, what I have learnt from him. Like Mary I can "treasure all these things and ponder them in my heart" (cf. Luke 2:19); ponder what it means to belong to the Christ-Church to be part of it, what that means to me; ponder, that is turn, all these things over and over in my heart, chat to him about them if I want, or just make a comment or two, ask a question or have a little joke. Even just pondering brings things home to me, makes them sink in deeper.

I don't even have to ponder. I don't have to listen. I can just rest in him in stillness. "Be still before the Lord and wait patiently for him" (Psalm: 37:7 RSV). There's a magic about stillness, just resting in the Lord and leaving him all the space he needs, for when I am still and silent his presence is all pervading. What this presence in me really means is a thing I can't fully understand. Jesus is timeless and placeless. His presence entirely fills the universe from its earliest awakenings to its final consummation. Then all things will be drawn together in Christ. Only those features of it that resist transformation will disintegrate in some way or another and be lost. Perhaps his presence in me follows something of the same pattern. He was there desiring me even before my mother knew that she had conceived a child. He loved me even before my mother knew me. He holds the whole of my life in his hands, pervading my whole being through and through, guiding, protecting, leading me on, bearing me up, even when exterior events seem to be going dead against me. He is there sifting and separating the various strands, turning away harmful strains, nourishing the wholesome. And all the while he is working in me he is glorifying God, praising in me and for me, gathering me up in his prayer, creating and saving the world in me. His work, yes, but mine also as he and I are one. And he knows already just when the time will be ripe to take me out of this life and transport me into everlasting happiness in eternal union with him in the beatitude of life in the Trinity.

Hand-in-hand with Christ I need never worry, never fear: "Yahweh guides a man's steps, They are sure, and he takes pleasure in his progress, He may fall, but never fatally, Since Yahweh supports him by the hand" (Psalm 37 [36]:23–4).

CHAPTER NINETEEN

Off-centre

When I was a teenager I fancied myself as a poet. That was because I once went in for an inter-school competition and won a prize. They gave me £1, all twenty shillings of it and, as that was a lot of money for a schoolgirl in those days, I thought I had come into money. The subject set for the competition was "Cities". I decided to write a sonnet. That, I thought, would look good, and I would only have to write fourteen lines. I don't remember them all, just the first four, and they went like this:

Each man the centre of his little sphere,
Alone among the crazy multitude,
Heeds not, nor is he heeded by those near.
A city is the greatest solitude.

I don't know why those four lines have stuck in my mind but I think it was a scandal that I was given a prize for expressing sentiments like that! I didn't see any of the other competitors' entries but I can only conclude that there wasn't much talent about. After all, what I was saying amounted to this: everyone is jolly selfish and self-centred. Nobody takes notice of anyone else but thinks they are all crazy anyway. So, although there are plenty of people, uninteresting people, about, we are all very lonely.

I was about to leave school and the fear of what the big, wide world might hold was obviously coming through. That was hardly a reason for giving me a prize, unless, of course, I was only telling the truth. I mean, are we all that selfish? Are we each the centre of our own little sphere? Perhaps this needs looking into.

The truth is that basically we are the centres of our own little spheres. That is inevitable as in the centre of myself is the "me-ness" of me, and in the centre of you is the "you-ness" of you. We are two entities totally different, totally separate, totally apart, and each has a centre which, for convenience, we shall call "self". This is true whether we consider the countless millions of "selves" who inhabit the earth, or the few who make up our immediate circle of "others". This apartness can be intolerable, insupportable loneliness. Insupportable, intolerable because each "self" is overpoweringly drawn to meet other "selves". In my poem I ignored this draw. I said that each self "heeds not, nor is it heeded by those near". No wonder I went on to speak of "solitude". "Searing loneliness" would have been a better expression.

This is the basic situation but it doesn't end there. There are such things as relationships. Much of the pain in life comes from striving to make relationships and all the difficulties that arise: the incompatibilities, the misunderstandings, the falling short, the false notes, the imperfections of our inbuilt communication systems etc. We yearn for union and at the same time we want to remain ourselves and to fulfil ourselves.

Actually this "draw" is only a reflected draw. In much the same way as the moon and the stars do not emit any light of their own but only reflect to us the light of the sun, so also the draw we feel towards other creatures, is only a reflection of a much more powerful, I might almost call it "magnetic", attraction. God made us and never lets go of us. God spoke and the Word of God brought creation into being. I have already said that all creation is, so to speak, the crystallized utterance of the Word of God, and that the Word returns to God (Isaiah 55:11). So we are created to return to God with the Word. Therefore, we are continually being drawn, irresistibly drawn, towards the Godhead. Often we mistake the source of this attraction and feel drawn to other creatures. This is because every grain of stardust reflects something of the divine Word that brought it into being, and we can mistake the reflection for the Creator and so make little gods for ourselves. Though if we understand our creature relationships rightly, and get the balance correct, they will draw us closer to God as they are intended to do.

We saw earlier (Chapter Six) that the highest concentration of the Word of God in creation, the central point, is Jesus, the man who is God, and it is he who is the magnetic centre – a kind of spiritual centre of gravity. (I know that this is just human language, and I can't insist too strongly that care must be taken not to take any inadequate human expression too literally when speaking of the Godhead. Our words are just shadows, vague images, to help us grasp just a little of the marvellous mystery that God is.) St Paul said: "He has let us know the mystery of his purpose. The hidden plan he so kindly made in Christ from the beginning . . . that he would bring everything together under Christ, as head, . . . And it is in him that we are claimed as God's own" (Ephesians 1:9–11). Jesus himself confirmed this when he said: "When I am lifted up I shall draw all things to myself" (John 12:32).

Now, what happens when we are drawn to him? It sounds rather like one big huddle, but that is not the case at all. It would be more true to say that we are drawn *into* him so that, in some sort, we become one with him. St Augustine heard Christ say to him in prayer: "You do not assimilate me but I assimilate you." Augustine was referring to Holy Communion but the point applies here as well. This is a very great mystery.

We used to speak a lot about "sanctifying grace" and I don't think we understood much what it meant. We must get behind words to find out what they really mean, otherwise we are just juggling with words and saying nothing. Now surely the mystery is this: each one preserves his or her own identity but, in some way, which we will not fully understand in this life, we are endowed with, suffused with, a share in the divine life itself. This is a momentous transformation, raising us up onto an entirely new level of existence, into a totally new sphere of life – the Christ-Life – drawing us into the Family of God. We become one with Christ, the Divine Word, Godself, but never becoming God, remaining ourselves. Christ becomes the centre of our lives, where before "self" was the centre. He becomes the hub, around which the whole of our lives revolve and are animated by, so that God looking at us sees, not so much the mere creature, perhaps a pretty inadequate, soiled and broken creature, but the image of Godself, the Word of God living in us.

This was God's initial intention when, "He made them in his image and likeness" (Genesis 1:27). This was the "Christification" we have already spoken of which, however, does not happen automatically, but depends on our own free choice. If we choose to be centred on Christ we will be well and truly "on-centre". If not, we will be sadly "off-centre", just the centre of our own little spheres, and very little, inadequate, puny, lonely spheres at that!

Christ is the centre and purpose of all creation. There from the beginning, in full force at the Incarnation, drawing all things to himself, extending throughout the universe both as regards time and space. Christ *is* creation: "There is only Christ: he is everything and he is in everything" (Colossians 3:11).

This is a tremendous thought. We must turn it over and over in our minds before we can grasp even a glimmer of its marvellous meaning. It is the Spirit who operates this transformation in us, and the Spirit also will help us to grasp a little of the meaning of the gift that is thus bestowed upon us: "You are my son (my daughter), today I have become your father" (Hebrews 5:5, Psalm 2:7).

CHAPTER TWENTY

Soap and Water

A great many children don't like washing or being washed. That, at least, is proverbial with small boys, but I had also to resort to a system of different coloured stars awarded to small girls who had, or hadn't, cleaned their teeth to my satisfaction.

Some parents make it worse by saying things like, "If you don't wash your hands before meals you won't be Mummy's little boy." Of course, in reality Sonny would be just as much Mummy's little boy, and she would love him just as much, even if he had just fallen into the pigswill, as she would if he were all clean and polished in his best Sunday suit. Certainly she might feel exasperated if he did fall into the pigswill, especially if it were in his Sunday suit, and she might administer a punishment if he had been told not to go near the swill, but it wouldn't affect her deep love for her child. What she would want to do would be to clean him up and that is what kids don't like.

Of course, Sonny might not be able to wash his own hands properly. He might seize the soap, slop water everywhere, make himself thoroughly wet and transfer a considerable amount of dirt onto the wallpaper. But the backs of his hands would still be as grimy as ever, not to mention his nails.

We are rather like Sonny in many ways. We often do silly things, make mistakes, quite awful ones sometimes, and then feel rather bad about it, a kind of niggling guilt and, like Adam and Eve in the Bible story, our first instinct is to avoid God, to get a bit further away from anything that has anything to do with God – the Church, for example – and hide, thinking that God mightn't like us very much now. The last thing we believe is that God's love for us doesn't depend on our being "good".

God's love for us is unconditional. If we have, so to speak, "fallen into the pigswill" God will want us to get cleaned up but that won't affect the deep love of the Creator for the creature. God loves us because God made us. "You love all that exists . . . for had you hated anything, you would not have formed it" (Wisdom 11:24–5). The cleaning up part is a bit of a difficulty for us. Our guilty feelings make us think that we should get cleaned up before we are fit to go near God again, so we keep away. The trouble is that we can't clean ourselves up, we only make things worse. Then what should we do?

First we must trust God, believe in God's immense love for us, and believe in the divine power and desire to put everything right, no matter how entangled our affairs might be. Then we should go to God and expose ourselves to the divine loving compassion (that's what God's mercy is all about) and ask to be made whole and clean.

That raises two questions. First, how do we expose ourselves to God's mercy – where do we find God? Secondly, will it hurt?

The first question first. An objection may immediately arise: I don't care for God very much. I'm rather afraid of God, can't I go to Jesus instead? Certainly Jesus seems to appeal to some people more than God does. God is up there somewhere and I'm not sure that God cares. God is someone I can't understand. God is too far away. But Jesus was one of us and lived and loved and worked and died as we do. He's a friend.

He is indeed! And Jesus is all that we could wish for in being just like us and so understanding us but, how on earth is he going to be any use to us if he isn't God? If he was only a man who died 2,000 years ago all we could say about him was that he was dead and buried and that's that. Well that is not that! "Jesus is Lord (divine) and is risen from the dead." He is alive today and is in our midst.

Well, where will we find this Jesus-God when we are in a mess and need to be cleaned up? If you have followed all I have been saying in this book, you will realize that Jesus lives in his Christ-Church. This is not just a sentimental notion but something very real: "Know that I am with you always; yes, to the end of time" (Matthew 28:20). His power to clean up the mess we make of our lives is present in a very special way in his priests, who continue his bridge-role. To them he said: "Those whose sins you forgive, they are forgiven" (John 20:23). They won't forgive what they don't know about, so we go and have a talk to them about it.

Some people may recoil here and say: "Why should I tell my sins to a priest?" Why not? If you accept that Christ lives in us and that you can meet him in others, it should be quite natural to meet him in someone who has been specially called and anointed to continue Christ's priesthood, Christ's redeeming priesthood. Besides we take our most intimate sickness to our doctor, why not take our spiritual illnesses to a doctor of souls? We human beings need to talk to someone about our problems. Even people who don't believe in God all agree about this, that's why there are so many psychiatrists about and counselling is so popular. God knew we had this need and so thought up the sacrament of reconciliation so that we could have that little chat in strict confidence *and* hear those wonderful words spoken in Jesus's name: "I forgive you your sins. Go in peace." Psychiatrists can't say that!

Mind you, it's not quite all as simple as that. I don't believe in a god who waves a magic wand. *Of course* God's forgiveness is immediate, even before we make the first move towards finding a priest to confide in, God has forgiven us. But this brings us to that second question: Will it hurt? Perhaps a little.

What I mean is that there may be some clearing up to do, it might take a little time. Some problems can be somewhat complicated and take a little sorting out. What will Sonny's mother do when she finds that he's fallen down in the newly tarred road, grazed his hands and knees and got tar and gravel in the wounds? She will clean him up but it may smart a bit. In my young days the bottle of iodine used to be got out on occasions like that, and it stung like mad. Fortunately more humane treatment has been found nowadays. Fortunately too, there is more understanding, sympathy and kindness than there used to be for people who get mixed up in all kind of messes. That is because we have a clearer understanding of God's love for us and eagerness to forgive, and also of our complete inability to help ourselves.

Even so it is still rather like Sonny's grazed knees. Even after they've been washed and soothing ointment has been put on, even after Mummy's hug and kiss, those knees may be sore for a while and the dressings may have to be renewed. So it may hurt a little, it may take a little time for everything to be sorted out, but it can be done. What I am saying is that no matter how big a muddle we may be in, how many mistakes we have made, if we go to Jesus humbly and say, "I'm sorry", God's forgiveness is guaranteed and the mess can be wiped away. "Come now, let us talk this over," says Yahweh, "though your sins are like scarlet, they shall be as white as snow" (Isaiah 1:18), "I have dispelled your faults like a cloud, your sins like a mist. Come back to me, for I have redeemed you" (Isaiah 44:22).

This is all very beautiful and consoling and we can't be grateful enough to Jesus for making himself available to us in this way. It is wonderful to think that we can meet Jesus in our fellow men and women, render him service and receive service from him through them. Just think, I can meet Jesus in the smile or tears of a child, in the love of a friend, in a helping hand given or taken, and in the blessing or words of absolution from a priest! This is what the Christ-Church is all about. We must turn this over in our minds to bring it really home to us, and ask Jesus to help us to get rid of our hang-ups and to get it right.

CHAPTER TWENTY-ONE

A Crumb of Bread

One day, soon after I first went to the Lebanon, I was on supervision duty in the children's dining room when a little girl dropped a small piece of bread onto the floor. To my surprise she hastily picked it up and reverently kissed it. I passed no remark but just noted the incident, wondering. A few weeks later a similar incident occurred. This time I commented upon it to a Lebanese sister. "Oh, yes," she said, "we respect bread. You must never throw it away and we always kiss it like that if it falls on the ground." Pressed further she explained that bread represented life, and also, it was used at Mass and became the Body of the Lord.

That, I thought, was a truly beautiful custom! A crumb of bread on the floor gathered up and revered because it represents life! Yes, life is a gift of God, something to be protected and respected. Something precious to be grateful for because we don't just exist like things but we are all VIPs in God's eyes and God has prepared such VIP treatment for us in heaven, such happiness, and it's for ever. To make sure that we get that prize God has given us a place in Jesus, the Word, the Son of God. Daughters and sons of God, we are members of the Body of Christ.

Let us then, like those little Lebanese children, respect bread, but let us, for far greater reason, respect life, God-given human life. So many lives are thrown away, accidentally, carelessly or wrongfully. Thrown away, cast down, and, like bread crumbs, swept away or trampled underfoot. Let us gather them up reverently whenever we can. Human life is so precious and is destined to be transformed into the divine – a transformation

Men and women inhabit this world, the work of the Creator. They till the soil and harness the forces of nature so that by the labour of all things created they may have food to sustain their God-given life. But the true life that God gives is greater than just their human life, needing bread. The higher, divine life, which is theirs as adopted daughters and sons of God, also requires nourishment, the Bread of Life. This Bread is the Body and Blood of Christ, that Jesus Christ the only Son of God who was sent into this world so that we might have eternal life. So God willed, for God so loved the world

that is sealed in our union with Christ that takes place so poignantly in the Eucharist.

It was a brilliant idea to use bread for the Eucharist – Christ's way of remaining personally and materially with us after his resurrection. But then, of course, God is brilliant. You can just imagine us racking our brains to invent something really spectacular or sophisticated if it had been left to us to think up an idea for this. But God chose something very simple, easily available, something we are all familiar with and couldn't possibly be afraid of, and yet at the same time something that so perfectly suggests and represents what it actually is – Life. "The bread of God is that which comes down from heaven and gives life to the world . . . I am the bread of Life" (John 6:33–5).

Also bread so exactly symbolizes Christ's position in the Universe . . . He is the centre, drawing all creation into himself. Bread, "fruit of the Earth and work of human hands" (Roman Liturgy) is made through the coming together of so many strands of the universe. Strands that can be traced back to those early seeds that appeared when the world first began to take shape. Those seeds were painfully ground by hand between two stones when our early ancestors first discovered that, mixed with water, that primordial element, and baked by fire, it could become a staple food, the "staff of life". Later, all over the world, the seeds were ground by wind power in those windmills that stood on hills near villages. Wind, water, fire, soil and seed all co-operating with the labour of human hands: farmers, millers, bakers, and today engineers, mechanics, lorry drivers and so many more, all combining their efforts to bring us our daily bread. Surely bread has a universal significance and Christ is the centre of the universe. And he chose to be in the midst of us in that, our other Daily Bread. "Give us this day our daily bread", both daily breads!

Bread features prominently in Scripture also. Erring humanity was told in the person of Adam, "With suffering shall you get your food from the soil . . . with sweat on your brow shall you eat your bread' (Genesis 3:17–19). Bread was also used in worship:

"You are to offer Yahweh a new oblation. You must bring bread from your houses to present with the gesture of offering" (Leviticus 23:17). The priest-king Melchisedek offered bread and wine as a thanksgiving sacrifice for Abraham's victory over his enemies (Genesis 14:18). Perhaps it was because bread was precious and essential to life and therefore represented life, that it was used in sacrifice.

The whole purpose of sacrifice is to express our total dependence on God. We give God something that stands for life and it is as if we were saying, "Our lives are in your hands." One particular form of sacrifice was the communion sacrifice, or sacred meal. Part of the offering was returned to the offerers who ate it, thus symbolizing their identification with the offering and their union with God and among themselves.

Jesus knew that these ideas were familiar to the people of his time and would be readily understood by them. He built on this when, on the point of offering himself in sacrifice for us, he took bread and wine and said: "Take this and eat, this is my body", and "Drink all of you from this for this is my blood . . . which is to be poured out for many for the forgiveness of sins" (Matthew 26:26–8). St Luke adds: "Do this as a memorial of me" (Luke 22:19). And that is exactly what we do when, at Mass, the priest repeats the gestures and words of Jesus. At the first Mass ever said was thus the bread and wine transformed into the body and blood of Christ. This is what we receive when we celebrate the Eucharist, when we receive Holy Communion. It's that mighty Word of God leaping down again each time, leaping down right into our personal, individual lives.

Jesus had already promised this and there's a marvellous chapter in St John's Gospel which tells us all about this. You should read the whole of St John, chapter 6, yourselves, here I shall just quote some of it.

Jesus answered: "I tell you most solemnly, it was not Moses who gave you bread from heaven, it is my Father who gives you the bread from heaven, the true bread; for the bread of God is that which comes down from heaven and gives life to the world."

"Sir", they said "give us that bread always."

Jesus answered: "I am the bread of life. He who comes to me will never be hungry; he who believes in me will never thirst . . . Yes, it is my Father's will that whoever sees the Son and believes in him shall have eternal life, and that I shall raise him up on the last day" (John 6:32–40).

And Jesus repeated: "I am the living bread which has come down from heaven. Anyone who eats this bread will live for ever: and the bread that I shall give is my flesh, for the life of the world."

That is really something to shout about. "Shout, and sing for joy . . . for great in the midst of you is the Holy One of Israel" (Isaiah 12:6 RSV).

The Holy One of Israel is indeed in our midst and we have every reason to shout and sing for joy, yet, strangely we don't seem to get very excited about it. Perhaps we should read and re-read those passages from St John's Gospel and ponder their meaning very seriously. Of course we will be hopelessly out of our depth. This is something we simply can't grasp just by our own efforts of reflection. We must ask for the gift of greater faith. "I do have faith. Help the little faith I have" (Mark 9:25).

Fortunately, Christ can get on with his work within us even if we don't get excited or shout with joy, even if we feel flat and dull and distracted. We don't have to *feel*, we just *know*, know that it is he who is coming to us. We *want* him to come, and take the trouble to put our house in order if it is not already in a fit state to receive him. It may be we need a little "soap and water" (Chapter Twenty).

Then Jesus will work in us his work of love: healing, purifying, strengthening, building, transforming, unifying and reconciling us to the Father. Each communion strengthens the bonds between us and Jesus and draws us more closely into his Body, the Mystical Body of Christ, the Christ-Church so that our lives are centred more and more exactly upon him, and his life flows ever more strongly through us.

This unifying process goes on, not only in each individual

man or woman who receives Jesus in Communion, but also draws us all more closely together among ourselves. After all, if I am drawn closer and closer to the centre by my union with Jesus, and you also are drawn nearer and nearer the centre in the same way, then we must be getting closer to each other. Any unwillingness to grow closer to others could be an obstacle to my growing closer to Jesus.

"There is only one God
There is only one King
There is only one Body
That is why we sing
Bind us together Lord, Bind us together,
With cords that cannot be broken.
Bind us together Lord, bind us together,
Bind us together with love."

('Bind us together', *Songs of the Spirit*, revised by Michael Irwin. Compiled by Damian Lundy, F.S.C., Kevin Mayhew Limited.)

CHAPTER TWENTY-TWO

Conkers

L ooking out across the garden at the big chestnut trees towering over the lawn I wondered how many of their shiny brown conkers would ever become trees. As I watched, a little grey squirrel bounded over the grass, picked up its prize and carried it off. "There's one conker that won't become a tree, anyway", I thought, and I felt rather sad. It was worse still when, watching a TV wild life programme, I saw a beautiful little fawn deer snapped up by a leopard, less than an hour after being born.

Poor little baby deer! Poor shiny brown conker! What unfulfilled lives they had led, lives broken off almost before they had begun. And I thought of those horrid magpies stealing eggs out of other birds' nests, eggs that were laid that baby birds might grow into big birds, fly through the air and fill the countryside with song. And all the thousands of other living creatures that meet a similar fate: animals, fish, birds, insects and seeds of all kinds. What a waste! What a dreadful want of fulfilment!

Of course, there is this about it – if every conker, acorn, nut or seed of any kind became trees and bushes, I don't know where we'd put our homes or highways, so dense would be the vegetation. And if every egg became a bird, and every newborn pup became a beast, and the young of every fish or crab or frog or buzzing fly grew to full stature and lived to reproduce its own kind, well, one thing is certain, there'd be no room on earth for you or me. Except, of course, if nothing preyed on anything else everything would die for want of nourishment and so being fulfilled would turn into being destroyed.

God has provided for a wonderful balance and, perhaps, being a means of sustenance for other creatures, is, in itself a form of fulfilment for conkers and other big or little creatures. The thing to marvel at is the lavishness, the profuse prodigality of God's creation ensuring the survival of all species.

All this is the way it is for beasts and birds and butterflies, creatures that have no personal awareness or power of thought, and no higher destiny of eternal life. But surely it is different in our case? Made as we are in the likeness of God, we have to develop all our potential. We must be fully ourselves. In other words, we *must* be fulfilled.

Nowadays we are very aware of this need for recognition and fulfilment, but what we are not always so clear about, is *what that fulfilment consists of.* What do we mean by fulfilment? How are we fulfilled? If we don't get this right we will just be juggling with long, psychological words, or following a will-o'-the wisp which leads to bitterness. Also, as we shall come to see, an excess of pursuit of self-fulfilment leads to self-destruction.

Let us consider the case of a teenager, girl or boy, a talented young person, one of those all-rounders who seem to be good at everything and can pick up prizes and trophies equally easily in academic or practical fields, in art, sport and science. In fact our young person may be compared to a tree with many chestnuts on it. When it comes to the choice of a career it is obvious that options have to be taken up and some things have to be dropped. A short list is drawn up – and conkers fall to the ground. A final decision is made – resulting in the loss of more conkers. So much talent wasted? No, but preference is given to the development and perfecting of one, to which the others are sacrificed. Fulfilment cannot be attained by pursuing a dozen different objectives all at once. That would lead to the dispersion of energies, the frittering away of gifts and opportunities, to fatigue, frustration, discouragement, and giving up. A total waste of talent!

The possibility of choice is part of the package we call "free will" which was given to us humans. Choice involves sacrifice, but nothing is lost. Sacrifice in one field brings gain in another. Sacrifice has not had a very good press. Neither has discipline. It suggests that our freedom is being limited, and freedom is, perhaps, our most cherished possession. Actually freedom won't work without discipline, any more than fulfilment will.

Take the Highway Code, for example. It certainly imposes a degree of discipline upon road users. If it didn't, our freedom to use the roads would be very reduced. Fulfilment is subject to this same discipline. Supposing I bought a car capable of doing 130 mph and I thought that, to be fulfilled as a driver, I must be free to do 130 mph anywhere and at any time I felt like it. Just imagine me, speeding along a 30 mph limit area at 130 mph, shoving other cars off the road, scattering cyclists to right and to left, scaring pedestrians out of their wits, running over dogs, and ending up being flung through my windscreen in a pile-up at a crossroads. When I came to in hospital (if I had the good fortune to come to at all), I might find the accident ward pretty full up, but I hardly think I would be feeling very fulfilled. No, once again, the excessive pursuit of self-fulfilment leads, not only to self-destruction, but also to the destruction of others.

In any case, destruction of others is another form of self-destruction. It is cutting off the branch that we are sitting on. In our selfishness we forget our solidarity with others and how much we depend one upon another. In society we provide openings and opportunities for each other, as well as formation, stimulation and means of advancement. When we begin to exploit one another, society is endangered and everyone with it, the exploiters as well as the exploited. We are a corporate body, the Human Race, and we sink or swim together.

There are different levels of fulfilment corresponding to the different levels of life that we have in us. The lowest level is that which we share with the animals. I once heard an athlete described as a beautiful animal. Of course that was not fair to the athlete as there is a lot more to athleticism than mere animal excellence or brute force (it would be following a red herring to discuss this here), but physical perfection or satisfaction, just for the sake of physical pleasure is animal. Sex just for pleasure is also animal, though, again, sex has far deeper relevance than animal pleasure (another red herring). Eating is another activity we share with the animals; but animals eat to live, and to make a god of one's belly is truly disgusting. Few, I would hope, seek fulfilment only on the animal level.

Then there is the human level. A human being has intelligence, power of thought, awareness of self, of others, of beauty etc. A human being has, too, imagination, foresight, calculation and free will. Many people seek fulfilment on this human level, and rightly so. And many are the success stories of humanity whether it is in industry, commerce, art, music, science, law or medicine etc. And many people are humanly fulfilled by being happily married and having lovely families. Possibly there are many, many people who consider themselves very fulfilled as human beings and think that this is quite good enough. Nothing is good enough except the highest, fullest possible life and if fulfilment stops halfway it is not only half fulfilment, it is half emptiness.

Every man, woman and child, at some time or another *knows* that somewhere within them there is an emptiness, an unfulfilled area. We are not often "still" enough to be aware of this and that God is offering us completion just in this area. "Be still and know that I am God" (Psalm 46 (45): 10 RSV). And so some of us show little or no interest in the higher Christ-Life that I have talked so much about and instead of seeking fulfilment on this higher, divine level there are those who say, "I'm not interested in religion. I don't believe in God. I am God as far as I'm concerned."

No level of fulfilment should be neglected but fulfilment merely on a human level, in human achievement, is worse than half empty, because it is doomed to decline and fade away. It is like the fulfilment of a dragonfly that lasts only a day. After all the toil and effort and worry that has gone into attaining human fulfilment in one field or another, even the greatest achievement bursts like a beautiful bubble and its finality is signed by the doctor, on the death certificate.

We were never meant to fizzle out like that! We are called to membership of a higher sphere, an everlasting destiny in the Kingdom of God. I repeat, we must seek human development and fulfilment. The Christ-Life does not negate human life, it perfects it, then rises above it.

Jesus was talking about this Christ-Life when he asked: "What is the Kingdom of Heaven like?" Then, in answer to his own question, he told the story of a man who was digging in a field and found a treasure. The laws about treasure trove were obviously different in those days from what they are now because he was able to buy the field and get the treasure. But to do so he had to *sell all he had* (Matthew 13:44). The sacrifice was well worth it so nothing was lost.

Sacrifice is always involved, but as we have seen, nothing is lost as a greater gain results. This is what Jesus meant when he said: "Anyone who loses his life for my sake will find it," and added, "what, then, will a man gain if he wins the whole world and ruins his life?" (Matthew 16:25–6). He might as well have said: "What will he gain if he fulfills himself in every possible human way and mucks up his chances of eternal happiness?" After all, the life he meant we would find was the higher life that we gain in union with Christ, that share in Christ's own divine life, in comparison with which all else disappears like colours when the sun goes down. It was in function of this life, the gaining, or rather the accepting, of this Christ-Life, that we were given free will and the possibility of making that choice, that option for Christ. "In his body lives the fullness of divinity, and in him you too find your own fulfilment" (Colossians 2:9).

CHAPTER TWENTY-THREE

Profit and Loss

Modern airports are very fascinating places. Every comfort is provided from lounges with easy chairs to restaurants, lifts, shops, etc. Also you can wander round looking at all kinds of interesting people or go up onto the roof to watch aircraft landing and taking off. I know people who go to an airport for a day out and thoroughly enjoy themselves. But nobody would think of an airport as a permanent place of residence. The whole idea of an airport is a place from where you set off on a journey to somewhere else.

You can't go on that journey and you'll never reach your destination if you won't board the aeroplane. When you come to think of it there's a bit of a risk involved in boarding an aeroplane and taking off to climb thousands of feet into the air. And there are things you can't take with you, they would be too cumbersome, too heavy, too dangerous or just impossible to move. For example, if you are going to settle in another country you can't take your house with you, or your garden. Your car could prove a problem and your pets likewise. No, in a case like that you would have to lose something: a beautiful view, friendly neighbours, a favourite club or what have you.

We are going on a journey. No residence is permanent here, but many things that surround us, and many of our possessions, are decidedly attractive and mean a lot to us. Perhaps someone reading this doesn't believe in God, or in an after life. I would say to that reader, you still can't make anything permanent, you will have to lose it all one day, the day your light snuffs out and you disappear into your black hole. Do you really believe it will end like that? I wonder if anyone really and truly believes that it will all end in a fearful waste like that? I wonder if people who believe like that ever have just a little doubt about it and a little wistful feeling of "perhaps, just perhaps", there is something else to it.

I would find that dismal creed very hard to accept. I greatly prefer the belief that we are going to settle in "another land" when this life is over, and that the "take off" begins right now. That is to say even in this world we begin to live the Christ-Life that will enable us to enter fully into the Trinitarian love-life in Heaven. We can't stay in the airport all our lives and suddenly find that we have arrived when we haven't even taken off, our passports aren't in order and we haven't bothered to get visas or tickets.

I've said several times in this book that it is all a matter of our own choice. So we can live a higher form of life in Christ or stay behind and miss the aeroplane. The "take off" does involve leaving something behind – a way of living, certain habits or frequentations, too much self-indulgence or something else that losing might hurt. But if we lose something it is so that we may gain more, much more, something of infinite value which bears no comparison to the paltry things we have to lose. The trouble is that they don't look paltry to us, they look all important, vital, as close to us as our own lives. Jesus knew that we had thoughts like that and he said: "Anyone who wants to save his life will lose it, but anyone who loses his life for my sake and the sake of the Gospel, will save it" (Mark 8:35–6). That looks like a sentence of contradictions but if you think about it a bit, it is clear enough. "For my sake and the sake of the Gospel" gives the clue.

The "Gospel" means "good news". The "good news", of course, is that "Jesus is Lord" and has made the Christ-Life possible for us so that our lives, our real lives, are assured. But many of the things that *seem* to make up our lives have to be left behind. Jesus himself, as man, lost his life so that we might have life. "He gave up his life for us" (1 John 3:16). "I have come so that they may have life and have it to the full" (John 10:10).

When a baby is baptized he or she gets a ticket into the Christ-Church. You might almost call it a conditional ticket, requiring to be endorsed later on, when the child is old enough to know what is involved and to take personal responsibility. If the child does not appreciate the possibility that is open to him or her, of being one with Jesus fully alive and so of being a son or daughter of God, then the child will not see the point of accepting the loss of anything that *looks* good. They will obviously choose that which looks the most attractive and end up being browned off, if not burnt up, with an excess of the wrong things. Hence the need for children to be taught and guided in matters religious and moral, just as much as in any other branch of their education. This in no way takes from them their liberty of choice when they reach an age when they are able to exercise it.

This world is attractive, certainly. It would have been totally unworthy of God the Almighty Creator to create a world that was not beautiful and full of wonderful things – things for our use, not for our misuse. But however wonderful this world, "Greater things than this you will see." So "loss" and "gain" are key words in our priority building. What am I willing to lose? What do I hope to gain?

I don't care much for the word "gain", it sounds rather grabbing and selfish. I wouldn't gain anything if it weren't given. It is offered. The question is do I consider it worth accepting? Do I realize the immense value of what is offered? Instead of "loss and gain" shall was say "loss and acceptance"? Of course, I'd accept anything good that is going, but I can't hold out my hands to receive if they are not empty. First, I must be ready to lose the lesser goods that fill my hands, then I will be able to accept the higher ones. Sometimes I will need quite a lot of faith to believe that these higher offerings *are* greater and to make the choice.

I am not saying that all the things I am calling "lesser goods" are bad in themselves. On the contrary, many of them are very good. For example wine is good, and so is money and sex

114

certainly is, but in excess and when misused they are not good at all. When a lesser good becomes an obstacle to a greater good then the loss of it must be accepted. The greatest of all goods is Christ and union with him. Such a union brings with it a promise of eternal happiness. St Paul said: "I believe nothing can happen that can outweigh the *superior advantage* of knowing Christ Jesus my Lord. For him I have *accepted the loss of everything*, and I look on everything as so much rubbish if only *I can have Christ and be given a place in him*' (Philippians 3:8–9).

Outside of Christ nothing, however good, is permanent. If we grip hold of anything too tightly we will sooner or later discover that, as a flower gripped in a child's hot hand will wilt and die, so also everything that we try to grasp and hold as our own will either lose its beauty and attraction or just slip from our hands. Be it power, money, position, fame, sex, success or whatever. We may hold these things as from God, as loans rather than gifts, and use them according to the plan of God for what they were intended to be used, and must be ready to hand them back whenever they may be asked for.

This book is not meant to be a book on moral theology so I won't expound on the details of how all this works out, but neither would I wish to give the impression that God's drawing us into the Godhead through Christ is just a cosy get-together, which God must accept on our terms and conditions and feel honoured. No, we are the honoured party and the terms and conditions are God's. And God is not mocked.

Mistakes we make, any number of them, and we will go on making them. But everytime, having turned away from God, we return humbly we can be more than sure of a warm welcome and truly fatherly hug. And if we will only stay with God we won't have to count on our own strength which is weakness really. Instead, as God told St Paul, we can count on God: "My power *is at its best in weakness*" (2 Corinthians 12:9).

CHAPTER TWENTY-FOUR

Aunt Sally

I know what some people would like to say to me: "If God is all that caring as you have been trying to make out, how come there is so much suffering on earth? How come thousands are dying of famine? How come that child was killed on the road and so many old pensioners are mugged, murdered and robbed in their own homes? How come a haemophiliac was given a blood transfusion and died of Aids? How come . . .? How come . . .? How come . . .?"

I am not going to put up a case in defence of God. God doesn't need any defending. It would be impertinent on my part, as a creature, to set about defending the Creator. No, that is not the way it is. It is *we* who are in the dock standing accused, not God, and we have to answer some questions.

How come, when God has provided us with a beautiful habitat which can produce enough food for every man, woman and child alive and still have a lot over, how come that all we do is stockpile food mountains and drink lakes until we don't know what to do with it all and yet thousands die of hunger?

How come we pay farmers to destroy, or dig in crops, and oblige them to breed fewer head of cattle and sheep because some of us have too much when others have nothing?

How come that there is so much greed among us that the few grab the big slice of the cake, and when a few crumbs of it are shipped off to feed the starving, a lot of it never gets through to those needing it?

That's all our fault, not God's, so how come we dare keep throwing the blame on God?

A cheap kind of sport at fun-fairs is shying things at an Aunt

Sally. I suppose it gets something out of a person's system to do that kind of thing – perhaps we try to get something out of our system, guilt maybe, by flinging blame at God. But it's not on.

And that child in the road accident, or perhaps it is a young mother or father leaving a family behind, or someone who is maimed or who gets brain damage. Well, how come there are irresponsible drivers, speed fiends, drunk drivers or drug addicts behind a wheel? When cars were first used the law obliged a man with a red flag in his hand to walk in front of them to warn people of the danger! That's gone! But perhaps some people think we should employ God to race along, like some kind of glorified cow-catcher, clearning the highways of vehicles, cycles, pedestrians and children so as to make way for murderous drivers to speed recklessly along at their will. Or it may be those who are just too negligent to keep their cars in a safe mechanical condition, or to have their eyesight tested, or to have medical checks on the condition of their hearts or blood pressure see no reason to blame themselves if accidents happen. That kind of attitude is too irresponsible for words and yet it would seem we can only find God to chuck the blame at.

How is it that the human race has grown so savage that old people get mugged, murdered and robbed in their own homes; that girls and women get assaulted and raped even in broad daylight; that husbands, wives and babies get battered; that there are régimes that survive by torturing their opponents; that people can destroy other people with drugs, drink, pornography, obscene literature or videos and much else, all of which runs diametrically against the way God told us to live so as to be happy here and hereafter? How come that individuals and nations are hell-bent on warmongering and, worldwide, terrorists get more violent by the day? How is it we have the nerve to blame God for the harm that comes to us as a result of all that?

Criminal misuse of God's gifts has been going on ever since the dawn of human life on earth. Ever since God gave us minds to think with and wills to make choices with, we have used these gifts to defy God's laws and upset God's plans. Small wonder

117

then, that all kinds of things went wrong in the laboratory of the universe, and nasty stinks were made where perfumes were intended. I am not a scientist, able to trace the cause and origin of all the different sicknesses and diseases that have plagued the human race all through its history and continue to do so now, but I have a shrewd suspicion that every one of our illnesses is one of those stinks that were never meant to be, but lurk menacingly in all the smog that we have created. And yet, if we do not flatly deny the existence of God, we blame Godself when we or our loved ones are afflicted by this or that disease. After all, even as simple a thing as overeating can bring on a heart condition, and whose fault is that?

Obviously we can hardly be blamed for natural catastrophes. It's not exactly people's own fault if they get struck by lightning, drowned by a tidal wave or carried away by a tornado (unless, of course, there's some degree of carelessness or imprudence involved). These catastrophes are commonly referred to as "acts of God". That's unfair, as God never stirred up a volcano, tornado or tidal wave with the express intention of causing suffering. The causes of such natural disasters are more the concern of scientists than theologians and, for all I know, may have their roots in some ages-old happenings in the history of evolution. For all practical purposes we can consider them as natural causes and effects, all part and parcel of the environment we live in and so often abuse. What I wrote about our acceptance of human causes and effects, I think, can also apply here, but, once again, don't let's make an "Aunt Sally" of God by calling them "acts of God".

Perhaps a little reflection on human lifespan would be helpful here, as well as a reminder that there is a better life to come – "Greater things than this you will see." No one is guaranteed any specific length of life. Some people get a very long trek and others only a short cut. We may wonder why, but get no answer. While some bitterly blame God, no one seems to notice our own inconsistency: in the medical world vast sums of money, technology, skill and endeavour are spent in the effort to prolong one precious little life while, perhaps in the next room, viable, precious little embryos are being deprived of life. Is that God's work or ours?

At this point we may ask ourselves what is our own outlook on "life", and what are our priorities. Have we set our priorities so strongly in favour of this world that we are not interested in life in the next as if there were neither Christ-Life nor Heaven? If so, that is rather a pagan attitude. We were not made for this world. We were made to share the love-life of the Trinity for ever and ever. This world is only the route there. St Paul reminds us of this when he has a word for when we are in the excruciatingly painful situation of losing someone we love. He says: "We want you to be quite certain . . . about those who have died, to make sure you do not grieve about them, like the other people who have no hope. We believe that Jesus died and rose again, and that it will be the same for those who have died in Jesus: God will bring them with him" (1 Thessalonians 4:13–14). Paul didn't say we weren't to grieve at all, that would be heartless. But not *like those who have no hope*, because we have hope of finding our dear ones again without fear of further separation. However painful bereavement may be, and indeed it is, we must remember that pain was never in the plan of God. As I have been saying again and again, pain and suffering have come into the world through the contrariness of the human race who, for generations and generations, over a period of untold thousands of years, has always thought that it knew better than God, even that God wasn't necessary – unless an "Aunt Sally" were needed – and that God's laws and directives could be pushed aside with impunity.

God could have left us to stew in our own juice. An uncaring god would have done just that. Instead, not wanting us to lose our way and miss the everlasting joy and happiness, peace and love of eternal life, God set about putting us back on course. The Word of God leapt down to make sure we can all get to the right destination. The journey may still be uncomfortable but the journey is of secondary importance. It's the destination that matters.

CHAPTER TWENTY-FIVE

Into the Depths

As the only way to try out a new prayer book is to pray it, I took the *Way of the Cross* I had been given to the chapel and proceeded to make the Stations of the Cross.

The first station – an innocent prisoner of conscience is unjustly put to death. The second station – a paraplegic or spastic person carries the cross of handicap. The third station – a long-term unemployed person cracks under the strain.

The whole spectrum of human suffering unfolded as the stations proceeded. It was all beautifully and sensitively portrayed and yet, somehow, I was not quite happy with that *Way of the Cross*. I turned to the Introduction and read that the Passion of Christ was being suffered in humanity today, and that was where our compassion should be, not in weeping over the sufferings of a man who died nearly 2,000 years ago. I was even more unhappy by this time, yet I could not deny that there was a degree of truth in what the author of the prayer book was saying, but it wasn't all the truth. I looked for a way of explaining to myself why I was unhappy.

It occurred to me that if I were shown a passport-type photograph of someone showing only the head and shoulders of the person, I would still have a good idea as to what that person looked like. If, on the other hand, the photograph gave a full-length likeness it would tell me a lot more. The person might be tall, healthy-looking and well-built, or a hunchback or, possibly, in a wheel-chair etc. But, no way would I be interested in a photograph showing a body without a head. This, it seemed to me, was what that *Way of the Cross* was doing. The man who was put to death nearly 2,000 years ago was the "head" without which the body does not make sense. And the sufferings of the body do not add up without the head.

Human suffering presents a terrible problem for us all. This has been the cause of much heartache and searching as well as of rebellion. A completely satisfactory answer is hard to find. For myself I have come up with these conclusions. First of all the deep-seated root cause of all human suffering lies in original sin (Chapter Fifteen). Secondly, God definitely *does not will* human suffering. Having given us the great gift of free will, God does not take it back, but lets human cause and effect take its course. This has gone on for so long that a lot of things have become "off-course". We can't expect, that is to say claim as a right, all kinds of miracles to prevent or alleviate suffering. What God *does will* is our response to cause and effect; that we accept it and "carry the cross" it often lays upon us. God is always ready to come to our aid and give us the strength and courage needed to carry our cross. Sometimes we do see God intervening more positively. The frequent "miracle" of peace and serenity, happiness even, that we often meet in people heavily weighed down by suffering is one of the most striking proofs of this.

There is another thing. Thanks to the fact that the Word leapt down into our midst and that, as man, Jesus took suffering to himself, not only do we suffer following in his footsteps, but as we have become one with him, our sufferings become those of Jesus. This gives all our pains and hurts an enormous value. As Jesus, the "head" suffered meaningfully – for our redemption – the suffering of the "members" of Christ's Body also become meaningful, they share the meaning of Christ's suffering. In fact this value is infinite. That makes sense of suffering, but (don't tell me, I know) it does not make it easier to bear. At the time of suffering, blind holding on in faith is all we can do.

Just one more thing. Suffering either makes or mars us. Our times of hurt can become our times of growth. Those who have never suffered do not know anything. We learn a lot through suffering. We grow stronger from enduring patiently. We become more understanding, tolerant and kindly. We lose many illusions about ourselves and grow humbler. We also learn to be more unselfish. We are purified, less weighed down by worldly ambitions, possessions and goals and so we can move more easily in the Christ-Life and eventually into heaven. Perhaps, to our surprise though we should have expected it, when we do arrive at our final destination, we will find that much that we had thought we had lost, or missed out on, will be waiting for us, and what we thought was God's hand hurting us, was, in reality the divine carer leading us home.

On the other hand, suffering rejected or rebelled against, can shrivel us up with self-pity and resentment, bitterness and hate, and finally destroy us as well as destroying others round us.

None of this will mean anything if we do not grasp the fact that the Word of God really did leap down into the depths of our human condition and identified with the whole of humanity. So every person, however crushed, broken or distorted they may be, however despised or rejected by other people, all are destined to be caught up into Christ, to share his divine life and to rise again with him. "He was first to be born from the dead" (Colossians 1:18). And we are to follow. That is our hope.

Then there is healing. Whole books have been written about the different kinds of healing. I would just say a word about the Sacrament of Healing. St James said: "If one of you is ill, he should send for the elders of the church, and they must anoint him with oil in the name of the Lord and pray over him. The prayer of faith will save the sick man and the Lord will raise him up again; and if he has committed any sins, he will be forgiven" (James 5:14–16).

We have taken that advice to heart and so we have what is called the Sacrament of the Sick. Unfortunately this is a very misunderstood ceremony. A lot of people look on it, and even call it, the "Sacrament of the Dying". As a result they do not call in the priest until the sick person is really on the point of death, and so, on the pretext of not frightening the sick person, they deprive him or her of so much help, strength and consolation, both physical as well as spiritual. At that point nobody expects the dying person to feel better and get up, and, of course, that doesn't happen. Nothing physical, at any rate, happens, though forgiveness of sin does take place and the sick person may be more at peace. But, on the whole, the sacrament is too often just looked upon as rather a formality, which it was never meant to be.

St James said "ill", not "dying", so ill is what is meant. That doesn't mean that for a cold in the head or a little indigestion we should ask a priest to anoint us, but any serious illness warrants recourse to the sacrament, and as promised, healing can be had. Plenty of people can witness to the remarkable power of the anointing and prayer of faith. In many cases total recovery has begun from that moment. In fact healing of one kind or another always takes place when a broken creature exposes his or her brokenness and hurt to the compassionate and powerful love of the Creator.

Healing can take place in many ways. Illness may go away and health be restored. Or it may be the spirit that is healed and the sick person may be filled with a deep peace and happiness. But there is another healing, deeper and more permanent, if we have faith to understand it like that. We cling so tightly to health, to life itself, as if there were nothing more to hope for. "Why are you so frightened, you men of little faith?" (Matthew 8:26). Homecoming is the great restoration that Jesus came down into the depths of our human condition to assure. "Behold I make all things new" (Revelations 21:5 RSV).

We often forget to think of death as a healing. Death *and* resurrection was the way the brokenness of Jesus was healed, and we will be healed that way too. "Just as all men die in Adam, so all men will be brought to life in Christ" (1 Corinthians 15:22); "And God will wipe away all tears from their eyes" (Revelations 7:17), for "Christ Jesus . . . abolished death, and he has proclaimed life and immortality through the Good News" (2 Timothy 1:10).

CHAPTER TWENTY-SIX

Fall-out

L et's make up a science-fiction story.

A new planet is discovered xxx million miles away from Earth. It is immeasurably superior to Earth in every possible way: superb scenery, perfect climate, excellent nourishment, no pollution, no viruses, germs or harmful microbes. You mention it, it has it in the superlative. And it is so big that everyone can go there. Of course everyone does want to go there.

New highly-superior spaceships are invented that can easily take people there, and there are as many flights as are required to meet the demand. Breathing and feeding on the journey are no problem because of new highly-perfected processes and, as for when people get to this new planet, they don't have to worry about life insurance policies, or anything of that sort, because, thanks to a simple injection of life-elixir before setting off, anything as unpleasant as death has been done away with.

Now, that's the setting. You'd think the story would have a happy ending. It does really but unfortunately there are just a few people (and you'd really wonder what possessed them!) who, just when the spacecraft was well on the way, got tired of the rather cramped quarters aboard and, bored with the flight regulations, decided that with their scientific knowledge they could quite easily make the journey on their own. They opened a hatch (labelled "keep tightly closed") and stepped out into space.

Of course, propelled by the momentum of the craft they had been travelling in, they continued for some time to float along in the wake of the ship they had left, but after a while different currents and magnetic forces began to pull them off course.

When the crew of the spaceship noticed what had happened they threw life lines to those outside. Some, already regretting their foolhardiness, grasped the lines and were pulled back to the safety of the craft. The others only sneered. For some time they weren't in the least alarmed. They seemed to be going more or less in the right direction and were confident in their powers. They thoroughly enjoyed their perfect freedom. Just imagine how marvellous it was to be delightfully floating along without a care or worry and without the least constraint. They scoffed at the spacemen in the ship and the sheep-like passengers cooped up inside.

However, a time came when they weren't so sure of themselves. By now the spaceship was miles away and out of sight. No longer were they going in the same direction that it had taken. They were drifting away from one another and darkness began to surround them.

Finally the awful moment came when they realized that they were astray in millions of miles of empty space, just whirling round and round in darkness orbiting some alien, smoke-covered sun. In a flash they knew that they could never, never reach the wonderful planet, neither could they return to Earth. There was nothing left for them but the dreadful, empty loneliness of endless and endless orbiting in that awful darkness. Thanks to the latest technology they could draw breath and nourishment from the surrounding element and, thanks to the life-elixir injection, they would never die. They panicked. They were petrified with fear. They flailed their arms and legs and tried to scream into the emptiness all around them but all to no avail.

That's the end of my science-fiction story. Fortunately it is only fiction and not true! But, just a moment, there may be some truth in it. To me that story is a picture of "exterior darkness" commonly called "Hell".

Readers may ask: "Do you really believe in Hell?" My answer is, "Yes, I do." However, I would qualify that answer by adding that I don't believe in the old-fashioned concept of flame and brimstone and of horrid horned devils with long tails and pitchforks. What I do believe in is the possibility, I say *possibility*, of falling out of Christ's orbit and so not making it into our heavenly destiny. That possibility is terrible and very frightening. It's the worst possible thing that could ever happen to a person and there is no reprieve.

The shattering thing about the sad ending of my story is that it *need not have happened*. It never should have happened and could so easily have been avoided. The astronaut piloting the spacecraft certainly didn't want anything like that to happen and tried to prevent it from happening. Those people had been warned and the notice was on the hatch. It was crazy of them to open the hatch door and jump out. It was entirely their own fault. Why ever did they do it?

I don't believe God sends anyone to Hell. Only those who freely choose to do so lose their way in that horrific fashion.

Jesus gave stern warning about the danger of eternal loss. He speaks in very strong language about a guest at a wedding party being thrown "out into the dark, where there will be weeping and grinding of teeth" (Matthew 22:13). He also told a parable about a king who will say: "Go away from me, with your curse upon you, to the eternal fire prepared for the devil and his angels" (Matthew 25:41–2). (See also Matthew 25:1–13 and Matthew 13:30.)

We can't dodge texts like that even if we don't like them. What are we to make of them? I think we can't take them standing alone but must look at them in the light of the whole Gospel. The predominant note of the Gospel, which comes across like the strong beat of the big drum is that *Jesus came to save not to condemn*. If he died for us, paid a very high price for us, he is not going to turn round and chuck us over. Time and time over in the Old as well as the New Testament we are told that God does not want the death of the sinner, but that he be saved. How then match this up with those dreadful texts I've just quoted?

The warnings of Jesus, like Yahweh's in the Old Testament,

were not given because he *wanted* anyone to be lost, or would cause them to be so, but because he was too honest just to be conning us. No, he was warning us because there is the *possibility*, and he didn't want it to happen. Please God it won't happen, has never happened. For all I know, nobody, absolutely nobody, has ever fallen out of the spaceship, at least not so far that they couldn't be pulled back. Please God, that's the way it is! Though, we must admit that some things are done around us that are so wicked that it almost makes you wonder if there is a Hell hot enough for those who do them. Perhaps that is what Jesus had in mind when he spoke of everlasting fire. But it was certainly as a warning to get people to change their ways.

If there is a dangerous possibility like that, we should know what would cause it to happen and how to avoid it. God gave us the commandments especially the two great commandments of love for this very reason. Involuntary ignorance will not cause anyone to be lost. We know that from Jesus's dying prayer: "Father, forgive them they *don't know* what they are doing" (Luke 23:34). If Jesus prays, his prayer is certainly granted, he is God as well as man. But there is such a thing as voluntary ignorance, just not wanting to know and deliberately shutting our eyes so as not to know unpalatable truths or rules of conduct. This is crass indifference. Then we have a way of thinking that we can get on without God, and trust in our own wisdom and powers and dispense with all regulations. Even without going that far, we often think that religion, too much of it, is rather a bore. We look upon life as a busy motorway full of traffic, commerce, politics, science or pleasure, etc. with religion running alongside like a little-used footpath. In reality the Great Business of life is going out to meet Christ. This should take up the whole of the road no matter what occupation we are engaged in or what interests we have. Everything should be done for the sake of the Kingdom. This in no way interferes with legitimate living or even pleasure. As St Paul says: "Whatever you eat, whatever you drink, whatever you do at all, do it for the glory of God" (1 Corinthians 10:31). Moses, speaking to the Israelites of long ago, said: "Understand this today and take it to heart. The Lord is God indeed, in Heaven above as on Earth beneath, he and no other. Keep his law and commandments as I give them to you today" (Deuteronomy 4:39–40). That is good advice. If we follow it there will be no danger at all of our losing the Christ-Life and spoiling our chances of reaching our heavenly destiny where, "Greater things than these we shall see."

CHAPTER TWENTY-SEVEN

Just Waiting

The little harbour was full of boats – big boats and little boats, sailing boats, rowing boats and dinghies. Tied to their moorings, they had all swung round nose into the breeze and were just gently, so very gently, bobbing up and down, doing nothing. Though thinking about it, I reflected that they weren't really doing nothing, they were waiting. Waiting is not the same as doing nothing. Doing nothing is aimless and empty. Waiting is full of expectancy. These boats were waiting for their owners to come and take them out to sea. That's what boats are for. Some would wait for hours. Others might wait for days or perhaps even weeks, but their owners had tied them up and left them there and they were awaiting their return. Patiently they were waiting, just waiting.

How much of life, I thought, is spent in waiting. I think I am doing nothing when I'm waiting. I may not be doing much, if anything, but the Lord may be doing a lot, and it's what the Lord does that matters. A mother pregnant with brand new life, can only wait. There is nothing whatever that she can do to bring her child to term before the appointed time. But while she is waiting the Creator is at work within her – making a human being.

The fishermen whose boats were waiting in the harbour were men used to waiting. They waited for the tide, for the wind, the sun, the rain and the seasons. They waited for the fish to rise. Sometimes they waited in vain and came home to port with empty nets. Like Peter, who had "laboured all night and caught nothing" (Luke 5:5). On that occasion Jesus had stepped in and told him to cast the net in once more and Peter caught a multitude of fish. It's what the Lord does that matters.

But when I'm waiting I think I'm doing nothing. I wait for a train, I wait for a letter. I wait for an opportunity, which perhaps never comes. In sickness I wait for health. I wait for next week, for next year – there's always a next! The child waits to grow up. Youth waits for maturity. Old age comes along and waits, just waits. The day will come when the call is heard, and "Blessed are those servants whom the Lord will find waiting" (cf. Luke 12:35–6). It is what the Lord will say that will matter.

Waiting is not a new experience in the history of the world. Evolution was a very slow process to start with, and the world waited and waited to become a fit habitat for humankind. And then it waited and waited for the first human beings to make their appearance. The waiting went on as they developed and progressed, until, finally God chose one man to found a nation with whom to make a Covenant, the nation from whom was to spring the Messiah, the One who would be sent, but that even was still a long, long way off. Centuries and centuries passed before "He who was to come", the Promised One, was born of Mary of Nazareth in the reign of Caesar Augustus (cf. Luke 2:1).

In the meantime the Israelites waited. In fact they were a waiting people. The expectation of the Messiah became more and more the central point of their spirituality. That doesn't mean that they were always and at all times conscious of the coming Messiah. In fact, probably there were long periods when the majority of the rank and file, and even the leaders, were completely ignorant of anything more spiritual than their crops and herds, as Jeremiah said, "Both prophet and priest ply their trade through the land, and have no knowledge" (Jeremiah 14:18 RSV). At one period the Book of the Law was mislaid. When it was found again it was like a new discovery (cf. 2 Chronicles 34:15–21).

Time and time over Yahweh sent prophets to rouse up the faith of the Chosen People, and, with their faith, their expectation of the accomplishment of the Promise, and once again they became an expectant, waiting people. We, like the

Israelites of old, are also a waiting, an expectant people. Though, like them, we all too often lose sight of the Promise, and are often scarcely aware of for what, for whom we are waiting.

Jesus promised that he would come again: "You will see the Son of Man coming on the clouds of heaven with power and great glory" (Matthew 24:30). "Therefore you must stand ready because the Son of Man is coming at an hour you do not expect" (Matthew 24:44).

I'm not going to try to tell you when this final coming of the Lord will happen, nor what form it will take, because neither I, nor anyone else knows. But we do know that it will happen and, what is more important, it will mean the final triumph of Christ over all the powers of evil. That is why we proclaim it so often: "Christ has died, Christ has risen, Christ will come again." We must think what we are saying when we make that proclamation because we may be tempted to be depressed on account of all the evil we see around us. We can see no hope for ourselves or for the generations to come outside of Christ.

God, we must remember, is not timebound as we are. God's horizons are infinitely wider than ours. "To God a thousand years are like a day: The Lord is not being slow to carry out his promises, as anyone else might be called slow; but he is being patient with you all, wanting nobody to be lost and everybody to be brought to change his ways" (2 Peter 3:8–9). God is waiting but, Christ, when he comes again will put all wrongs to right. God will be glorified and God's wisdom, power and holiness will be proclaimed in the view of all creatures. This will be a magnificent day, not only for God but also for us. We will share in Christ's resurrection, glory, triumph and everlasting joy as we have become one with him. Therefore we should never forget that we are a waiting people.

We may think that we are doing nothing while we are waiting, but if we understand what being one with Christ really means, and open ourselves to him and allow him to, he will live in us, pray in us, work in us, and perhaps suffer in us, bringing to

131

completion the work he began at Bethlehem, Nazareth and Calvary, in fact from the beginning of time, "master craftsman" that he has always been. Oh yes, it's what the Lord does that matters.

The final coming may be very spectacular. The Big Bang that started everything could have been very spectacular, and what we are told about the end suggests that it will be spectacular. "The coming of the Son of Man will be like lightning striking in the East and flashing far into the West" (Matthew 24:27). ". . . the sun will be darkened and the moon lose its brightness and the powers of heaven will be shaken. And then they will see the Son of Man coming in the clouds with great power and glory" (Mark 13:24–6). "The Day of the Lord will come like a thief, and then with a roar the sky will vanish, the elements will catch fire and fall apart, the earth and all it contains will be burnt up . . . the sky will dissolve in flames and the elements melt in the heat (2 Peter 3:8–13). (See also Luke 17:24, 21:25–8; 1 Thessalonians 4:16.) I couldn't say how much of this we should take literally and how much is symbolical. I think much is symbolical, but whichever way it is I think we can conclude that it will be a very special day, unlike any other we have known.

You and I were not there to see the Big Bang but we do experience its effects. We may not be there to see the final coming of the Lord either. Our personal final encounter with him may be sooner than that. Actually he is coming all the time, and the more we are on the look-out for him in these daily comings, the greater will be our joy when our final Big Moment approaches. It should be a moment to look forward to, not to fear. St Peter speaks of us "waiting and longing for the Day of the Lord to come" (2 Peter 3:12). Let us then welcome him in the events of our daily lives, even in disappointments, sickness and pain.

Sickness and pain, the forerunners of death, tell us that our luggage is being sent on in advance. As a friend awaiting us on the railway platform, steps into the carriage and takes out our cases one by one, so Jesus steps into our lives and takes things that are ours – our health, our strength, our hearing, eyesight, mobility, our memory and more, and we, lacking faith fear that they are being taken away for good, and fear to let them go. In truth it is to facilitate our disembarkation at our destination that our luggage is taken off in advance. Then, with empty arms, we can freely throw ourselves into his embrace and "death becomes a communion" (*Le Milieu Divin*, Teilhard de Chardin), and not only a communion but the beginning of an ecstasy that never ends, and all our waiting will be over.